Elaichi
Cardamom

Kali Mirch
Black Pepper

Jeera
Cumin

Dalchini
Cinnamon

Methi
Fenugreek

Saunf
Fennel

Rai
Mustard

Lavang
Clove

Kalonji
Onion seeds

INDIAN FLAVOR

Dhania
Coriander

NDIAN FLAVOR

CURRY LEAVES, CUMIN SEEDS
ND THE SPICE OF HEALTHY COOKING

JEETI GANDHI

PHOTOGRAPHY BY **DIRK PIETERS**

FOOD STYLING BY **ABIGAIL DONNELLY**

LAUREL
GLEN

San Diego, California

Laurel Glen Publishing
An imprint of the Advantage Publishers Group
5880 Oberlin Drive, San Diego, CA 92121-4794
www.advantagebooksonline.com

First published in the UK in 2002 by
New Holland Publishers (UK) Ltd
Garfield House
86–88 Edgware Road
London W2 2EA
United Kingdom
www.newhollandpublishers.com

1 2 3 4 5 06 05 04 03 02

ISBN 1-57145-864-6

Library of Congress Cataloging-in-Publication Data available upon request.

All notations of errors or omissions should be addressed to Laurel Glen Publishing, editorial department, at the above address. All other correspondence (author inquiries, permissions, and rights) concerning the content of this book should be addressed to New Holland Publishers (UK), Garfield House, 86–88 Edgware Road, London W2 2EA, United Kingdom www.newhollandpublishers.com

Publishing manager: Linda de Villiers
Managing editor: Cecilia Barfield
Editor: Catherine Murray
Designer: Petal Palmer
Assistant designers: Sean Robertson
   and Beverley Dodd
Photographer: Dirk Pieters
Food stylist: Abigail Donnelly
Proofreader and indexer: Pat Barton
Reproduction:
   Hirt & Carter Cape (Pty) Ltd
Printing and binding:
   Craft Print PTE Ltd, Singapore

CONTENTS

INTRODUCTION

A few months ago, while I was at a party, I overheard a discussion on Indian cuisine. Some of the comments made are still vivid in my memory. One of the women said, "To make any dish taste Indian, I just add curry." "But curry is so hot and spicy. I never enjoy eating it," another replied. Then someone else complained that although she loved Indian curry, it was too rich and oily for her liking. Yet another, who seemed to enjoy cooking, said that her family loved Indian food and she would love to cook it at home, but she was put off by the fact that it seemed so time-consuming, and it was her impression that not all the spices were readily available. Though I was happy to hear that people loved Indian cuisine, I couldn't help feeling that most of the comments I'd overheard were sadly unjustified.

On another occasion I hosted a large dinner party for several friends and business associates. From appetizers to dessert, every dish was Indian. For convenience I labeled each dish with its name and a brief description of the ingredients. When dinner was served, I noticed that most guests served very little of each dish on their plates (perhaps they didn't know what to expect). However, within the next few minutes I noticed some of them returning to the table for seconds, with very flattering comments like: "I have never tasted anything so delicious and full of flavor"; "You don't get food like this in Indian restaurants"; "Would you mind giving me some of these recipes?"; and "Are all the spices you need available here, or do you get them from India?"

That evening so encouraged me that I decided to compile a cookbook full of delicious and easy-to-prepare Indian recipes, along with basic information about Indian food and traditions, for my friends who enjoy Indian cuisine and would like to cook it at home.

I have also been inspired by a friend who, despite a strict vegetarian diet, has enjoyed many nutritious, well-balanced vegetarian meals at my home. Worldwide, more and more people are turning vegetarian, either because of medical advice or by choice. A common complaint is that vegetarian food can become monotonous, and it is difficult to find recipes with the right nutritional balance, particularly of protein. This book should fill that gap by providing plenty of nutritious and delicious vegetarian recipes.

Indian cuisine is a unique combination of different spices and herbs with meat, fish, seafood, vegetables, legumes (lentils, beans, and peas), paneer (homemade fresh cheese), and yogurt. Certain recipes require one or two spices only, while more elaborate ones may need eight to ten or more spices to obtain the desired flavor. It is therefore correct to say that Indian food is "spicy," but not always "hot" or "pungent." The only spice that makes Indian food hot is green or red chili peppers, chopped or in powdered form. These can either be totally eliminated or the amount adjusted according to taste without affecting the flavor of the dish. The amount of other spices used in the recipes can also be altered according to taste. If you prefer a pungent taste, add extra chili pepper or hot chili powder.

Do not be put off by long lists of ingredients. Once you have the recommended list of spices on your shelf, along with any others required by the recipe, every dish will be simple to prepare and delicious to eat.

As I come from northern India, most of the recipes in this book are from that region and a special effort has been made to avoid the use of unhealthy ingredients. Ghee (clarified butter), cream, and butter have been used sparingly or replaced by unsaturated vegetable oil.

So go ahead and try some of my recipes, and surprise your family or friends with a delicious, home-cooked Indian meal. I can assure you that, without exception, they will taste far better than the so-called Indian food made by simply adding curry powder to a dish!

FROM LEFT TO RIGHT: TURMERIC, GREEN CHILI PEPPERS, CILANTRO, BABY EGGPLANT

Regional and cultural differences in Indian cuisine

Religion has a great influence on the food habits of Indians. Hinduism has been the predominant religion for centuries, and most high-caste Hindus do not eat meat, fish, or poultry. There are those who may eat only fish. Beef is strictly forbidden for religious reasons. Cow slaughter in certain states of India is prohibited, as Hindus consider the cow a sacred animal and a great provider. People from other faiths, such as Muslims, may eat all types of meat except pork, while Christians have no such prohibitions.

India is a vast country that is divided into many states and different territories. Apart from the geographical and regional divides, there are, as mentioned above, the religious and cultural differences. There are numerous languages and dialects spoken, and almost every region has its own culinary tradition and style. A north Indian meal will be totally different from a typical south Indian meal, for example. The Mogul invasion of India during the sixteenth century had a great impact on food habits, particularly in the northern Indian states. Hence northern cuisine, including Mongolian specialties, are strongly influenced by central Asian cuisine. North Indians love rich food and tend to use more cream, ghee, and nuts in cooking, a trend that is, of course, changing as people become increasingly health-conscious. They prefer to grind their spices and prepare different masalas (spice mixes) at home.

Coastal states in the east have an abundance of fish, and consequently fish is preferred over other meats. The cooking medium is mustard oil, whereas in the western and southern coastal regions more coconut and coconut oil are used in cooking. The use of tamarind juice to impart a subtle sour taste to various dishes is also common.

In Rajasthan and part of Gujarat (desert areas), a great variety of legumes, dehydrated vegetables, and preserves such as pickled vegetables are used in cooking owing to the nonavailability of many fresh vegetables.

The only common factor linking these diverse cooking traditions is the use of spices to create endless aromas and flavors typical of the Indian kitchen.

How to serve and eat Indian food

Traditionally, Indians eat three main meals: breakfast, lunch, and dinner, as well as afternoon tea (very British). In some communities, breakfast and lunch are combined (brunch), followed by a light snack in the afternoon and then dinner.

A typical Indian meal consists of a dish with gravy (commonly known as "curry"), be it meat or fish, or for vegetarians, legumes or paneer (homemade cheese). In addition, there will be a vegetable dish, plain yogurt or raita (yogurt with vegetables such as cucumber, spinach, or tomatoes), and rice or chapati (Indian bread made with whole-wheat flour) or both, plus some chopped-up salad with lime juice dressing or green chutney, and pickles.

FROM LEFT TO RIGHT: WHOLE CLOVES AND WHOLE NUTMEG, SAFFRON, STAR ANISE, GROUND MASALA

GROUND, DRIED CHILI PEPPERS

Generally, there aren't different courses in an Indian meal as in a typical Western meal, with the exception of dessert or Indian candies, which may be served separately after the meal. Little dishes that are often served with tea in the afternoon, and many other Indian dishes, are not confined to a particular meal and can be served with lunch, dinner, or simply as a snack. This, however, is changing, and people like to serve snacks with cocktails or as appetizers before a meal when entertaining.

Traditionally, food is served in steel, silver, or other metal plates called *thalis*. Small metal bowls, or katories, are placed in a thali for yogurt preparations and wet dishes. Cooked food is usually placed in serving bowls on the dining table. Everyone then serves their food into their individual thalis and katories. Alternatively, food is served in individual thalis from the kitchen and brought to the table, a tradition still followed by many orthodox Indian families. Diners may be seated on the floor on mats or rugs and the thalis placed in front of them on individual low tables. Many serve food on banana leaves and in plates and bowls made with leaves of the banian tree. This practice is most prevalent during religious ceremonies and weddings, especially in southern India.

Garnishes are simple, such as chopped fresh *dhania* (fresh cilantro leaves), onion rings or slices, green chili peppers, and lemon slices or wedges. Yogurt dishes are garnished with chili powder, black pepper, or ground cumin.

Food is usually eaten with the fingers. A small piece of chapati is broken and wrapped around some meat or vegetable and then eaten. Even rice is usually mixed with wet dishes or yogurt and neatly eaten with the fingers. With Western influence, however, the old traditions are disappearing, and more and more people these days are using dishes and table utensils.

I have provided serving suggestions with most of the recipes to help you to prepare a typical Indian meal for your family or when entertaining. Feel free to mix and match East with West. Serve an Indian dry vegetable dish with roasted or grilled meat or fish. Eat bread or rolls with Indian meat dishes instead of chapati or rice. Serve vegetable, meat, or rice pulao with a tossed salad or plain yogurt, and so on. Be adventurous and try as many dishes as possible!

Useful tips to make life easier

Preparing some of the most frequently used ingredients in Indian dishes can be very discouraging. If you would really like to enjoy Indian meals more often and save time and energy, I have a few suggestions to make. These have proved very helpful to me, especially when I was living on my own.

The most important tip is to read the recipe carefully and make sure you have all the ingredients in stock. Prior to starting the actual cooking, measure out and prepare the ingredients according to the instructions, and only then start to cook.

Onions, garlic, and ginger

In most recipes, these three ingredients are frequently used, and processing them every time you want to cook a dish can be time-consuming. I therefore do the following:

INDIAN FLAVOR

Onions

As and when time permits, grind extra onions in the food processor and brown them in oil. If the fat content is a consideration, use a small quantity of oil, add a little water to keep the onions from burning, and stir frequently. Heat the oil over high heat in a nonstick pan. Add onions and reduce the heat slightly. Fry, stirring occasionally, until golden brown. Cool, then divide into portions (depending on the recipes you want to try in the future), place in small containers or plastic bags, and freeze. This preparation is suitable for dishes with gravy. Remember the appearance and texture of anything with gravy will depend on how well the onions are browned.

Similarly, minced onions can be sautéed and frozen for making dry vegetable balti preparations and legume dishes.

Garlic and ginger

These ingredients are available in paste form in most supermarkets. Personally, I prefer to make my own as the flavor of freshly prepared paste is far superior—even after freezing—and it contains no preservatives.

I buy 7 ounces of each and soak them separately in sufficient water for at least 4–5 hours or preferably overnight, as this makes peeling much easier. Grind them separately in the food processor to a smooth paste. Use a few drops of water if necessary. Cut aluminum foil into 3-inch-square pieces. Drop a teaspoon of garlic or ginger paste onto each piece and fold it into a small pocket. Place them all in a box or freezer bag, label, and freeze.
Thaw when needed.

Masala

Preparing your masala (page 122) in advance will save you from having to do all the preparations at once.

Cilantro (dhania)

In the preparation of Indian cuisine, there is no substitute for cilantro. It is readily available in most supermarkets.

Unfortunately, it does not stay fresh for very long. To make sure I always have it on hand, I buy an extra quantity, wash it, cut off the roots, mince it, and then freeze it in an airtight container. It is not necessary to thaw it before using.

Paneer

Paneer is a most versatile ingredient and can be prepared in a variety of ways in a short time. I always make paneer (page 119) using at least 5 quarts of milk, and freeze it. Freezing does not affect the quality or the taste. Simply cut paneer into small cubes, place in two or three freezer bags, and freeze.

Cooking extra quantities

Save time and effort by cooking an extra quantity of your favorite dish and freezing it for later use. Most Indian dishes can be frozen for months without losing their flavor. Potatoes are the only exception, as they do not freeze well. Any frozen Indian food should be thawed completely before reheating.

Approximate equivalents

When dealing with food in the kitchen, I find it rather difficult to work with very precise weights and measures. Slight inaccuracy in measuring sometimes occurs and is permissible, as long as it is close to the specified quantity. Try to use a set of standard measuring spoons and cups.

Measure	Is equal to
1 teaspoon	60 drops
3 teaspoons	1 tablespoon
4 tablespoons	¼ cup
8 tablespoons	½ cup
12 tablespoons	¾ cup
16 tablespoons	1 cup
2 cups	1 pint

APPETIZERS

The concept of serving appetizers in Indian homes is a comparatively recent trend, borrowed from the Western world. Nowadays it is an integral part of Indian cuisine and all sorts of snacks are served with cocktails or as the first course of a meal.

Most of the recipes in this section can also be served as accompaniments to main dishes, as a snack between meals, or as a light meal. Served as a snack between meals, the dishes will obviously go further than if they were served as appetizers.

The tandoori dishes in the following chapter can also be served as appetizers, particularly the kabobs.

AND SNACKS

ALOO CHAAT
POTATO CANAPÉS
MAKES 12 PIECES

2 medium potatoes, peeled, cooked,
and cut into very small cubes
½ cup bean sprouts
(chopped if shoots are long)
1 tablespoon minced onion
1 tablespoon chopped cilantro
1 small green chili pepper, minced (optional)
1½ teaspoons ground cumin

½ teaspoon kala namak (optional)
½ teaspoon pepper
½ teaspoon hot chili powder (optional)
1 teaspoon sugar (optional)
3 tablespoons lemon juice
12 slices hothouse cucumber, ½ inch thick, with peel
mint sprigs, to garnish

In a bowl, mix together the potatoes, bean sprouts,
onion, cilantro, and chili. In another small bowl
place all the dry spices, sugar (if used), and lemon
juice, and mix thoroughly. Add to the vegetables
and toss well. Adjust seasoning to taste. Place the
cucumber slices on a platter, top each with a
spoonful of *chaat,* and garnish with a mint sprig.

TIP
Can be prepared in advance. Cover with plastic
wrap and refrigerate until needed.

CHANA BHAJIA
FRIED CHICKPEA SAVORIES
SERVES 12

14-ounce can chickpeas (garbanzo beans)
1 egg
¼ cup flour
½ teaspoon cumin seeds
1 teaspoon ground cumin
½ teaspoon hot chili powder
salt, to taste

½ teaspoon baking powder
2 tablespoons minced onion
1 teaspoon ginger paste
1 small green chili pepper, seeded and minced
(optional)
3 tablespoons minced cilantro
vegetable oil, for deep-frying

Drain the chickpeas in a strainer and rinse briefly
under running cold water. Place the chickpeas, egg,
and flour in a blender and blend until a slightly
coarse paste forms. Add a tiny bit of water if it is
too thick to blend. The consistency should be like
thick cake batter. Pour into a mixing bowl. Add the
remaining ingredients, except the oil, and adjust
the seasoning.

Heat enough oil to fry the *bhajia* in batches over
medium heat. Using two teaspoons, drop the batter
in small amounts into the hot oil. Using a slotted
spoon, turn the bhajias a few times. Fry until golden
brown and cooked through. Drain off the extra oil
on paper towels.

Serve hot on toothpicks, with pudina chutney
(page 123) or tomato sauce for dipping.

CHANA BHAJIA

ALOO CHAAT

BAINGAN KACHRI
SPICY EGGPLANT SLICES
MAKES ABOUT 12 SLICES

1 tablespoon lemon juice
½ teaspoon salt
2 tablespoons vegetable oil
1 large eggplant, cut into ½-inch-thick slices
1 medium onion, minced
1 teaspoon minced garlic
1 small green chili pepper, seeded and minced (optional)
1 tablespoon coriander seeds, pounded
1 tablespoon cumin seeds, pounded
salt, to taste
1 large tomato, chopped
2 tablespoons chopped cilantro
½ teaspoon black pepper
1 teaspoon dry mango powder or 1 teaspoon lemon juice
mint leaves, to garnish
cherry tomatoes, halved, to garnish

Mix together the lemon juice, salt, and 1 tablespoon of oil. Brush on both sides of each eggplant slice. Broil until tender and light brown. Keep warm.
In a nonstick frying pan, heat the remaining 1 tablespoon of oil over medium heat. Add the onion, garlic, and green chili pepper (if using), and sauté until translucent. Add the coriander, cumin seeds, and salt, and sauté for a few seconds more. Stir in all the remaining ingredients and cook until the tomato is just heated through (do not overcook). Top each eggplant slice with the cooked mixture and garnish with mint leaves and cherry tomatoes.
Serve as a first course or as a side dish with any main dish of your choice, with chapati (page 98) or rice.

SABZI PAKORA
VEGETABLE FRITTERS
MAKES ABOUT 60 FRITTERS

vegetables
1 green bell pepper, seeded, cut vertically into ½-inch-thick pieces
1 small eggplant, sliced into ½-inch-thick pieces
1 cup small cauliflower florets
1 medium potato, peeled and cut into thin rounds
12 small, tender leaves of spinach
12 baby corn ears, slit in half lengthwise
vegetable oil, for deep-frying
batter
2 cups gram flour* or all-purpose flour
½ teaspoon turmeric
½ teaspoon baking powder
½ teaspoon cumin seeds
1 teaspoon ground cumin
½ teaspoon hot chili powder, or to taste
salt, to taste
1 teaspoon garlic paste
½ teaspoon ginger paste
water

Pat the vegetables dry with a paper towel and set aside.
To make the batter, sift the flour into a bowl. Add all the remaining ingredients except the water. Gradually add the water, stirring well to make a thick batter, rather like pancake batter.
Heat the oil in a deep pan or wok. Dip a few vegetable pieces in the batter to coat them completely, then deep-fry in hot oil until golden brown. Do not fry too many *pakoras* at once, as this will reduce the oil's temperature and make the pakoras soggy and oily. It is advisable to fry each type of vegetable in separate batches.
Drain on paper towels. Serve hot with pudina chutney (page 123).

*In India we use gram flour (*besan*) for making pakoras, but all-purpose flour can be used. Any Indian grocer will stock gram flour. It gives a very subtle flavor to this dish.

ALOO SOYA TIKKI
POTATO AND SOY BURGERS
MAKES 16 SMALL PATTIES

½ cup TVP (textured vegetable protein) granules*
2 medium potatoes, cooked and peeled
2 slices whole-wheat bread
2 tablespoons minced onion
3 tablespoons minced cilantro
1 teaspoon minced fresh ginger
1 small green chili pepper, seeded and minced (optional)
1½ teaspoons ground cumin
1 tablespoon cornstarch
½ teaspoon garam masala (page 122)
1 tablespoon lemon juice
salt, to taste
vegetable oil, for deep-frying

Prepare the TVP granules (see page 120) or follow the instructions on the label. Set aside. Chop the potatoes coarsely and place in a mixing bowl. Soak the bread slices in water and immediately squeeze dry. Crumble into the mixing bowl with the potatoes and mash with a potato masher. Add all the remaining ingredients except the oil. Adjust the seasoning and divide the mixture into sixteen equal portions. Shape into small patties (*tikkis*). Heat the oil and fry 4–5 patties at a time until golden brown. Serve hot, garnished with onion rings.
Serve with yogurt pudina chutney (page 123) or with tomato or peri-peri sauce.

*As a substitute for TVP granules, add 1 extra potato and ¼ cup each of chopped cooked beans and carrots instead.

TIP
The tikkis can be fried ahead of time. Keep uncovered in a single layer in a warm oven until ready to serve. They will stay crisp. Make larger tikkis and serve with a green salad for a light lunch.

MACHHI AMRITSARI
SPICY FRIED FISH
SERVES 6

Amritsar is a city in northern India, where this dish is a specialty.

14 ounces fish fillets (any firm white fish)
1 teaspoon ginger paste
1 teaspoon garlic paste
1 teaspoon fresh lemon juice
2 teaspoons tandoori masala (page 122)
½ teaspoon salt
3 tablespoons all-purpose flour
3 tablespoons cornstarch
1 teaspoon garam masala (page 122)
1 teaspoon ground cumin
½ teaspoon carum seeds (optional)
½ teaspoon pepper
½ teaspoon hot chili powder or cayenne pepper
salt, to taste
vegetable oil, for deep-frying

Cut the fish into pieces just smaller than 2 inches square and place in a mixing bowl. Rub with the ginger, garlic, lemon juice, tandoori masala, and salt. Set aside.
   In a small plastic bag, mix together all the remaining ingredients except the oil. Place 3–4 pieces of fish in the bag and shake well to coat each piece with the flour mixture. Remove the coated pieces and repeat with the remaining pieces of fish.
   Heat the oil in a wok or deep pan. Fry the fish in batches until crisp and golden in color. Drain on paper towels and keep warm. Serve as soon as they are all fried.
   Serve plain or with dahi pudina chutney (page 123). The fish can also be served as a main course with dal, kheera pudina raita (page 75), and rice, or with mashed potatoes and a salad of your choice.

PANEER CHAAT

PANEER CHAAT
SPICY HOMEMADE CHEESE
SERVES 8

8 ounces low-fat paneer cubes (¾ inch each)
1 teaspoon ground cumin
½ teaspoon toasted ground cumin (page 122)
1 teaspoon ginger juice
½ teaspoon black pepper
½ teaspoon hot chili powder
2 tablespoons minced cilantro
1 teaspoon granulated sugar
1 tablespoon lemon juice
salt, to taste

Place the paneer cubes in a mixing bowl. Add the cumin, ginger juice, pepper, and chili powder. Set aside. Place the cilantro and sugar in a mortar and grind with a pestle until the sugar is crushed. Add the lemon juice and salt. Stir in the paneer mixture and mix gently.

Serve on toothpicks on a bed of lettuce leaves.

MAKKI KE PAKORA
SPICY CORN FRITTERS
SERVES 8

2 cups frozen corn kernels
2 tablespoons minced onion
2 teaspoons minced fresh ginger
1 small green chili pepper, seeded and minced (optional)
2 tablespoons minced cilantro
1 teaspoon ground cumin
1 teaspoon paprika
salt, to taste
1 egg, well beaten
½ teaspoon baking soda
¾ cup all-purpose flour
vegetable oil, for deep-frying

Place all the ingredients, except the oil, in a mixing bowl and mix thoroughly. If too thick and dry, add a little water to get the consistency of a thick paste.

Heat sufficient oil in a wok, or any other suitable pan for deep-frying, over high heat until a drop of corn mixture fries quickly. Now drop in the mixture by the spoonful (6–8 at a time) and fry until deep golden in color. Remove with a slotted spoon and place on paper towels to drain.

Serve hot with dahi pudina chutney (page 123).

TAND

There is a great variety of dishes that can be listed under this section. Different kinds of meat, fish, paneer, and vegetables can be cooked tandoori-style. One characteristic common to most is the use of yogurt, ginger, and garlic, though the combination of spices may differ.

Kabobs and tikkas are terms generally used for a variety of small pieces of meat cooked in a tandoor, on an open fire, grilled, or fried. The most important characteristic of good kabobs or tikkas is that they should be lightly charred on the outside, succulent inside, and should almost melt in your mouth. Overcooking can spoil the flavor and make them dry and chewy.

Yogurt marinade helps to tenderize meat to an extent, but is not enough to achieve the desired texture when it is cooked. For convenience, I generally use a commercially available meat tenderizer—unripe papaya is the best and most effective. Peel and grind it, then add to a yogurt, ginger, and garlic marinade. Most kabobs and tikkas should be left to marinate for six to eight hours or preferably overnight. This helps to tenderize the meat so well that it requires only a little cooking. Always select prime cuts of meat for the best results.

Most meats and fish with tandoori marinade can be frozen for several weeks. Bring to room temperature before cooking. Leftover marinade can be mixed with oil and used for basting during the last five to seven minutes of grilling.

Most tandoori dishes can be served as appetizers or with a main meal, and the size of servings adjusted accordingly. Serving suggestions at the end of each recipe give various serving options. All types of kabobs can be used as a filling for rolls or pita bread.

FROM THE
OOR

MURGI KA TIKKA

CHICKEN TIKKA

SERVES 6 AS AN APPETIZER OR 3 AS A MAIN COURSE

14 ounces boneless chicken, cubed
1 tablespoon vegetable oil, for basting
marinade
¾ cup plain, low-fat yogurt
1 teaspoon ginger paste
2 teaspoons garlic paste
2 teaspoons fresh lemon juice
1½ teaspoons tandoori masala (page 122)
1 teaspoon garam masala (page 122)
1 teaspoon hot chili powder, or to taste
salt, to taste

First make the marinade by mixing together all the marinade ingredients in a bowl. Add the chicken cubes and stir through until they are thoroughly coated in marinade. Cover and marinate in the refrigerator for 5–6 hours or preferably overnight.

Bring the marinated chicken to room temperature before cooking. Thread the chicken pieces onto skewers. *Braai* (grill) or broil, turning and basting every few minutes, until cooked through but still juicy (about 15–20 minutes).

Serve the chicken pieces on toothpicks instead of skewers, with pudina chutney (page 123) as an appetizer or as a main meal along with a legume dish, a vegetable dish, chapati (page 98), or rice and raita.

MURGI MALAI KABAB

CREAMY CHICKEN KABOBS

SERVES 6 AS AN APPETIZER OR 3 AS A MAIN COURSE

14 ounces boneless chicken, cubed
1 tablespoon vegetable oil, for basting
marinade
2 tablespoons almond paste (page 123)
3 tablespoons cream
1 tablespoon garlic paste
2 teaspoons ginger paste
¼ teaspoon ground mace
¼ teaspoon grated nutmeg
½ teaspoon hot chili powder, or to taste
½ teaspoon pepper
2 teaspoons cornstarch
1 tablespoon minced cilantro
salt, to taste

First make the marinade by mixing together all the marinade ingredients in a bowl. Add the chicken and mix well. Cover and marinate in the refrigerator for 5–6 hours or preferably overnight.

Bring to room temperature before cooking. Thread the chicken pieces onto skewers. Grill or broil, turning and basting every few minutes, until cooked through but still juicy (about 15–20 minutes).

Serve the chicken pieces on toothpicks instead of skewers, with pudina chutney (page 123) as an appetizer, or as a main meal along with a legume dish, a vegetable dish, naan (page 105) or chapati (page 98), and raita.

MURGI KA TIKKA

TANDOORI MURGI

SEEKH KABOB

TANDOORI MURGI

TANDOORI CHICKEN

SERVES 4

4 small chicken drumsticks and 4 thighs,
or 4 skinless, boneless breast halves
1 teaspoon hot chili powder, or to taste
2 tablespoons lemon juice
½ teaspoon salt
2 tablespoons vegetable oil, for basting
marinade
¾ cup plain, low-fat yogurt, whisked
2 teaspoons ginger paste
1 tablespoon garlic paste
1 teaspoon garam masala (page 122)
1½ teaspoons tandoori masala (page 122)
salt, to taste

Separate the drumsticks from the thighs or cut each breast into two pieces. With a sharp knife, make 2–3 deep slits on both sides of each piece. Set aside.

Mix together the chili powder, lemon juice, and salt, and rub over each piece of chicken. Set aside for 10–15 minutes.

Meanwhile, prepare the marinade by combining the yogurt, ginger and garlic pastes, garam masala, tandoori masala, and salt. Coat the chicken pieces with the marinade, cover, and refrigerate for 5–6 hours.

Bring to room temperature before cooking. Grill or broil, turning and basting every few minutes, until cooked through but still juicy (about 15–20 minutes).

Serve with dal, such as tarka dal (page 59), roti or naan (page 105), and dahi pudina chutney (page 123), with mashed potatoes or French fries, sautéed vegetables, and a green salad. Garnish with onion rings and lemon wedges.

TIP

Prepare extra and freeze to prepare makhni murgi (page 40).

SEEKH KABOB

SHISH KABOBS

MAKES 8 KABOBS

10 ounces (1¼ cups packed) lean ground lamb
1 teaspoon minced, fresh ginger
2 teaspoons minced garlic
1 small onion, minced
2 tablespoons minced cilantro
1 small green chili pepper, seeded and
minced (optional)
2 teaspoons lemon juice
2 teaspoons tandoori masala (page 122)
1 teaspoon garam masala (page 122)
1 tablespoon cashew nut paste (page 123)
salt, to taste
8 wooden or metal skewers
2 tablespoons vegetable oil
2 tablespoons chopped fresh mint

Preheat the broiler to very hot or use a charcoal grill if available.

In a bowl mix the ground lamb with all the other ingredients except the oil and chopped mint. Divide this mixture into eight equal portions. Wrap each portion around a skewer in the shape of a hot dog. Brush each kabob with a little oil, then broil or grill, turning frequently, until done (about 15 minutes). Serve hot, garnished with chopped mint, as part of a main meal.

Alternatively, remove the meat from the skewers, cut the kabobs into bite-size pieces, and serve on toothpicks as an appetizer, with yogurt pudina chutney (page 123) on the side.

TIP

The kabobs can be prepared and cooked ahead of time. Cover with foil and keep in a single layer in a warm oven until ready to serve.

VARIATIONS

Ground chicken or beef can be used instead of lamb.

BOTI KABOB
LAMB KABOBS
SERVES 6 AS AN APPETIZER OR 3 AS A MAIN COURSE

14 ounces boneless lamb, cut into 1-inch cubes
2 tablespoons vegetable oil, for basting
marinade
¾ cup plain, low-fat yogurt
2 teaspoons ginger paste
2 teaspoons garlic paste
1½ teaspoons tandoori masala (page 122)

1 teaspoon garam masala (page 122)
1 teaspoon hot chili powder, or to taste
1 teaspoon raw mango powder or
  1 teaspoon lemon juice
meat tenderizer, used according to label instructions
salt, to taste

First make the marinade by mixing together the marinade ingredients in a bowl. Add the lamb and mix well. Cover and marinate in the refrigerator for 5–6 hours or preferably overnight. Bring to room temperature before cooking. Thread the lamb pieces onto skewers. Grill or broil, turning and basting every few minutes, until cooked through but still juicy (about 15–20 minutes).

Remove from skewers and serve on toothpicks with pudina chutney (page 123) as an appetizer, or as a main meal along with a legume dish, a vegetable dish, naan (page 105) or chapati (page 98), and raita.

VARIATIONS
Pork or veal are excellent substitutes for lamb.

TANDOORI LAMB CHOPS
SERVES 6

12 medium, lean lamb chops
2 tablespoons vegetable oil, for basting
marinade
¾ cup plain, low-fat yogurt
1 tablespoon ginger paste
1 tablespoon garlic paste
1 tablespoon minced fresh mint leaves

2 teaspoons tandoori masala (page 122)
2 teaspoons garam masala (page 122)
1 tablespoon lemon juice
1 teaspoon hot chili powder, or to taste
meat tenderizer, used according to label instructions
salt, to taste

First make the marinade by mixing together all the marinade ingredients in a bowl. Add the lamb chops and mix well. Cover and marinate in the refrigerator for 5–6 hours or preferably overnight. Bring to room temperature before cooking. Grill or broil, turning and basting every few minutes, until done (about 15–20 minutes).

Serve with a legume dish, a vegetable dish, naan (page 105) or chapati (page 98), and kachoomber raita (page 79).

BOTI KABOB **(TOP)** AND TANDOORI LAMB CHOPS **(BOTTOM)**

STUFFED BANGARA (GOAN-STYLE)
STUFFED MACKEREL
SERVES 4

The west-coast town of Goa, with its sun-kissed beaches, was ruled by the Portuguese for almost four centuries, and today Goan food still retains its strong Portuguese influence. This dish and vindaloo (page 49) are among my favorites. Both are very spicy and pungent, so I have modified them to suit a Western palate.

4 medium mackerel
1 tablespoon vegetable oil, for basting
lemon and tomato slices, to garnish
stuffing
5 large garlic cloves
½-inch-thick slice fresh ginger
1 tablespoon cumin seeds
1 tablespoon coriander seeds
1 teaspoon hot chili powder, or to taste
6 whole peppercorns
3 tablespoons malt or cider vinegar
2 tablespoons dry coconut cream
3 tablespoons minced cilantro
1 teaspoon sugar
salt, to taste

Clean and rinse the mackerel, and pat dry with paper towels. Cut along both sides of the bone (from the fin side) from head to tail to open like a pocket for filling. Set aside.
Place all the stuffing ingredients in a blender and blend to a smooth paste. Fill the fish with a little paste on either side of the bone. Brush with a little oil and grill or broil, gently turning once, until brown on both sides.
Garnish and serve as an appetizer or as a main dish with rice and a legume dish.

TIRANGA PANEER TIKKA
BARBECUED TRICOLOR CHEESE
MAKES 8 SKEWERS

1 teaspoon garam masala (page 122)
1 teaspoon ground cumin
1 teaspoon ground coriander
½ teaspoon fenugreek seeds, ground*
½ teaspoon hot chili powder
½ teaspoon pepper
salt, to taste
1 teaspoon ginger paste
1 teaspoon garlic paste
¼ cup plain yogurt
1 tablespoon vegetable oil
1 tablespoon lemon juice
10 ounces paneer, cut into 1¼-inch cubes
1 large red bell pepper, seeded and cut into 1¼-inch squares
1 large green bell pepper, seeded and cut into 1¼-inch squares
8 long wooden skewers

In a large mixing bowl, combine all the ingredients, except the paneer and peppers, and beat until smooth and creamy. Add the paneer and peppers and mix gently until they are well coated. Thread equally onto eight skewers, alternating paneer and pepper pieces. Grill or cook under a hot broiler, turning frequently, until the peppers just start to brown.

As an appetizer, serve on toothpicks instead of skewers, along with pudina chutney (page 123). For a perfectly balanced meal, serve with or without skewers, along with any dal, roti or rice, and a little aloo raita (page 79) on the side.

*Use a mortar and pestle to grind to a powder.

SOYA KABOB
SOY CHUNK KABOBS
SERVES 4

1 cup TSP (textured soy protein) chunks
8 wooden skewers
vegetable oil, for basting
marinade
¼ cup plain yogurt
2 tablespoons lemon juice
1 teaspoon ground cumin
½ teaspoon garam masala (page 122)
salt, to taste
1 teaspoon tandoori masala (page 122)
½ teaspoon hot chili powder
¼ teaspoon grated nutmeg
2 teaspoons garlic paste
1 teaspoon ginger paste

Prepare the TSP chunks (see page 120) and set aside. Place all the marinade ingredients in a bowl and whip to mix thoroughly. Add the prepared TSP chunks and mix to coat them well. Cover and marinate for 2–3 hours or more, turning the chunks over once.

Thread equally onto eight skewers and grill or cook under a hot broiler, turning frequently and basting with any leftover marinade and oil, until the chunks are golden brown.

Serve on toothpicks instead of skewers as an appetizer, along with pudina chutney (page 123). For a main meal, serve with or without skewers with any dal, chapati (page 98) or rice, and a little palak raita (page 76) on the side.

Fish holds an important place in an Indian meal. Both seafish and freshwater fish are popular, and any firm white fish is suitable for the recipes in this chapter. I generally use sole or hake, with very satisfactory results. Good-quality fresh shrimp, squid, and other fresh seafood are best for the recipes provided here. However, frozen, cooked shrimp and other frozen seafood can also be used with fairly satisfactory results. Thaw frozen seafood completely and pat dry before cooking.

North Indians tend to favor fried fish dishes, while those living along the coast prepare excellent dishes with rich gravies using coconuts and coconut milk. As fresh coconut is not always available, I have substituted dry coconut cream in the recipes. Canned coconut milk and coconut cream are available at large supermarkets or at any Asian market.

Most of the recipes given here are from northern India, with a few from the south.

ote

member that the color of dishes with gravy will largely depend on how well you
own the onion without burning it. Use nonstick pans to minimize the use of fat
hen sautéing or browning meat and onions, or keep sprinkling with a little water
keep onion, ginger, and garlic paste from sticking and burning. If you enjoy
ngent food, replace the paprika with hot chili powder according to taste. Oil
n also be used in place of unsalted butter without compromising the flavor.

FISH
AND SHELLFISH

TAMATER WALI MACHHI
FISH IN TOMATO GRAVY
SERVES 6

1¼ pounds firm white fish fillets
2 teaspoons ginger paste
1 teaspoon garlic paste
1 teaspoon lemon juice
1 teaspoon salt
½ teaspoon hot chili powder or paprika
1 tablespoon dry coconut cream
¾ cup water
1 tablespoon coarsely chopped cashew nuts
2 teaspoons sunflower seeds
2 tablespoons vegetable oil
1 tablespoon minced garlic
½ teaspoon turmeric
1 teaspoon ground cumin
1 teaspoon paprika
1 tablespoon tomato paste
2 large, ripe tomatoes, puréed
1½ teaspoons garam masala (page 122)
¼ cup minced cilantro
salt, to taste
¼ cup cream

Cut the fish fillets into small pieces (a little smaller than 2 inches each). Place in a mixing bowl and add the ginger and garlic pastes, lemon juice, salt, and chili powder or paprika. Mix thoroughly and let marinate for 30–40 minutes.

Soak the dry coconut cream in the water for 5 minutes. Place the cashew nuts, sunflower seeds, and coconut liquid in a blender and blend until a smooth paste is formed. Set aside.

Heat the oil in a pan over medium heat. Add the garlic and sauté for a few seconds without letting it turn brown. Add the turmeric, cumin, paprika, and tomato paste. Stir-fry for another 30–40 seconds. Stir in the coconut paste and continue stir-frying for 2–3 minutes longer. Add the fish, stir, and cook gently until the fish is well coated with sauce. Stir in the puréed tomatoes, garam masala, half of the cilantro, and salt. When it starts to bubble, reduce the heat to low, cover, and cook for about 10 minutes or until the fish flakes easily with a fork. Using a slotted spoon, remove the fish pieces to a serving dish and keep warm.

Add the cream to the remaining sauce in the pan. Stir and cook until the sauce starts to bubble again. Remove from the heat and pour the sauce over the fish. Garnish with the remaining cilantro.

Serve with plain boiled rice and kachoomber raita (page 79) or any other salad of your choice. The fish can also be served with plain Italian bread instead of rice.

DAHI WALI MACHHI
FISH IN YOGURT SAUCE
SERVES 6

1¼ pounds fish fillets (any firm white fish)
2 teaspoons garlic paste
1 teaspoon ginger paste
3 tablespoons lemon juice
1 teaspoon salt
1 tablespoon coriander seeds
1 tablespoon cumin seeds
6–8 large garlic cloves
¾-inch piece fresh ginger
1 small green chili pepper, seeded and minced (optional)

½ cup chopped cilantro
1 tomato, coarsely chopped
2 tablespoons vegetable oil
1 large onion, minced
½ teaspoon hot chili powder, or to taste
1 teaspoon mustard powder
½ teaspoon turmeric
1½ teaspoons garam masala (page 122)
salt, to taste
1 cup plain, low-fat yogurt, whisked
1 tablespoon chopped cilantro, to garnish

Wash the fish, cut into pieces a little smaller than 2 inches, and pat dry. Place in a mixing bowl with the garlic and ginger pastes, lemon juice, and salt. Mix well and set aside for a few minutes.
In the meantime, heat a small, shallow pan over medium heat and dry-fry the coriander and cumin seeds until brown, but not burned. Remove from the heat and allow to cool.
Place the garlic cloves, ginger, chili pepper (if using), cilantro, tomato, and browned seeds in a blender and blend until a smooth paste is formed (add a little water if it is too dry). Set aside.
In a nonstick pan, heat the oil over medium heat. Add the onion and stir-fry until golden brown. Stir in the blended paste, all the dry spices, and salt. Stir-fry for 1 minute longer. Add the fish and continue stir-frying for another 4–5 minutes or until the fish is nicely coated and has changed color. Reduce the heat to as low as possible. Stir in the yogurt and continue stirring gently until the sauce starts bubbling. Cover and cook over low heat for about 10 minutes or until the fish flakes easily with a fork. Garnish with cilantro.
Serve with plain boiled rice, kachoomber raita (page 79) or any other salad, and bread.

NARIAL WALI MACHHI

COCONUT FISH

SERVES 6

1¼ pounds fish fillets (any firm white fish)
3 tablespoons lemon juice
1 teaspoon salt
2 tablespoons dry coconut cream
½ cup canned coconut milk
½ cup water
4 teaspoons coriander seeds
2 teaspoons cumin seeds
4–5 large garlic cloves
¾-inch piece fresh ginger
1 small green chili pepper (optional)
1 teaspoon sugar
2 tablespoons vegetable oil
1 large onion, minced
1 large tomato, grated
1 teaspoon paprika
½ teaspoon turmeric
1 teaspoon ground cumin
1 tablespoon malt or cider vinegar
salt, to taste
2 teaspoons chopped cilantro, to garnish

Rub the fish with the lemon juice and 1 teaspoon salt, and set aside. Place the coconut cream, coconut milk, and water in a blender and let soak for 5 minutes. Add the coriander and cumin seeds, garlic, ginger, chili pepper (if using), and sugar. Blend to a smooth mixture. Set aside.
Heat the oil in a nonstick pan over medium heat and sauté the onion until golden brown. Stir in the tomato, dry spices, and vinegar. Stir-fry for 3 minutes. Add the coconut mixture and bring to a boil. Reduce the heat to very low and add the fish. Cover and cook for about 10 minutes or until the fish flakes easily with a fork, lightly stirring the sauce occasionally. Add salt, if necessary. Garnish with chopped cilantro.
Serve hot with plain cooked rice and a salad or raita of your choice.

BALTI MASALA JHINGA

SPICY STIR-FRIED SHRIMP

SERVES 6

2 tablespoons vegetable oil
1 tablespoon unsalted butter
2 medium onions, sliced
5 garlic cloves, minced
2 tablespoons tomato paste
2 teaspoons cumin seeds, pounded
2 teaspoons coriander seeds, pounded
1 small green chili pepper, seeded and minced (optional)
1 teaspoon garam masala (page 122)
½ red bell pepper, seeded and cut into thin strips
½ green bell pepper, seeded and cut into thin strips
1½ pounds raw shrimp, shelled and deveined
salt, to taste

Heat the oil and butter in a frying pan or wok over medium heat. Add the onions and garlic, and sauté until translucent. Add the tomato paste and all the spices, and stir-fry for 1–2 minutes.
Stir in the peppers and sauté for a minute longer. Add the shrimp and stir-fry for 4–5 minutes or until the shrimp have turned pink and are cooked through. Do not overcook. Add salt to taste and remove from the heat.
Serve as an appetizer or as a main course with a legume dish, a side dish of vegetables, and paratha (page 101).

INDIAN FLAVOR

SAMUNDRI KHAZANA
SEAFOOD IN ALMOND SAUCE
SERVES 6

2 tablespoons vegetable oil
1 tablespoon unsalted butter
2 large onions, minced
1 tablespoon garlic paste
2 teaspoons ginger paste
3 tablespoons tomato paste
2 large tomatoes, grated
¼ cup almond paste (page 123)
¼ teaspoon ground mace
2 teaspoons ground cumin
1 teaspoon turmeric
½ teaspoon hot chili powder, or to taste
1 teaspoon paprika
1 teaspoon garam masala (page 122)
salt, to taste
7 ounces raw shrimp, shelled and deveined
7 ounces calamari (squid) rings
7 ounces fish fillets, cut into small cubes
3 cups hot water
2 tablespoons minced cilantro

Heat the oil and butter in a nonstick pan over medium heat. Add the onions and sauté until golden brown. Stir in the garlic and ginger pastes, and stir-fry for 30 seconds. Add the tomato paste, grated tomatoes, and almond paste. Continue stir-frying for 1 minute longer.

Stir in all the spices, the salt, and all the seafood. Stir-fry for another 2–3 minutes. Add the water and half of the chopped cilantro. Bring to a boil. Cover, reduce the heat, and simmer for 5–7 minutes or until the fish flakes easily with a fork. Remove from the heat and transfer to a serving bowl. Sprinkle with the remaining cilantro and serve hot.

Serve with gobi aloo (page 68), onion rings dressed with lemon juice and salt and pepper to taste, and chapati (page 98) or rice.

TIP
This recipe freezes very well.

CHICKEN
AND LAMB

Nonvegetarian Indians like to have at least one meal a day that includes a fish, chicken, or meat dish. A few years ago, chicken was fairly expensive in India and was usually prepared only for special guests. Fortunately this has changed now, owing to the increasing number of chickens in India. Apart from tandoori dishes, there are many other wonderful ways of cooking chicken, and I had a hard task shortlisting recipes to include in this section. In the end I decided to provide simplified recipes that are easy to prepare, yet delicious to eat. Remember to pick smaller birds for more succulent results.

Hindus do not eat beef for religious reasons, and pork is forbidden for Muslims. Goat meat is very often the red meat of choice, and it is commonly available. Lamb and mutton are also used for many dishes.

Meat is generally cut into small pieces and cooked with the bone left in. The recipes in this section, for the most part, call for boneless meat, chops, or ground meat.

In northern India, meat is cooked with vegetables such as potatoes (a great favorite), spinach, turnips, or green peas.

MAKHNI MURGI

TANDOORI CHICKEN IN BUTTER SAUCE

SERVES 4

1 recipe tandoori murgi (page 25)
2 tablespoons unsalted butter
2 tablespoons garlic paste
1 tablespoon ginger paste
¼ cup tomato paste, mixed with ½ cup water
½ teaspoon ground fenugreek seeds*
1 teaspoon garam masala (page 122)
1 teaspoon paprika
½ teaspoon ground black pepper
½ teaspoon granulated sugar
salt, to taste
2 teaspoons minced cilantro
½ cup cream, mixed with 1 cup water
1 tablespoon chopped cilantro, to garnish

Prepare the tandoori murgi chicken and keep it warm. Heat the butter in a large, nonstick frying pan over medium heat. Stir in the garlic and ginger pastes and sauté for a few seconds. Stir in all the rest of the ingredients, except the cream and water mixture and the chopped cilantro. Stir and cook for 1 minute, then stir in the cream mixture. Bring to a simmer. Add the cooked chicken and cook while stirring gently for 2 minutes or until heated through. Transfer to a serving dish and garnish with chopped cilantro.
Serve hot with naan (page 105) or chapati (page 98), a vegetable side dish, and kachoomber raita (page 79).

* Gives a very subtle flavor to this dish.
Omit if you do not have it in stock.

MURGI KA KORMA

CHICKEN IN FRIED ONION AND YOGURT SAUCE

SERVES 4

vegetable oil, for frying
2 onions, thinly sliced
1 cup plain, low-fat yogurt
¼ cup ricotta cheese
2 tablespoons slivered almonds
2 onions, minced
2 teaspoons garlic paste
2 bay leaves
6 cardamom pods, cracked
1¼-inch piece cinnamon stick
1 teaspoon ground cumin
pinch of grated nutmeg
½ teaspoon pepper
½ teaspoon hot chili powder or 1 teaspoon paprika
½ teaspoon garam masala (page 122)
salt, to taste
8 skinless chicken legs, thighs, or breast halves
2 cups hot water

Heat sufficient oil in a round-bottomed pan or wok over medium heat. Fry the sliced onions until golden brown and crisp. Spread over paper towels to drain off the excess oil. Place the yogurt, ricotta cheese, almonds, and fried onions (saving a few to garnish) in a blender and blend to a smooth paste (add a little water if it is too dry). Set aside.
In a large, nonstick pan, heat 2 tablespoons of oil (use the same oil in which the onions were fried) over medium heat. Add the minced onions and sauté until golden brown. Stir in the garlic paste, all the spices, the garam masala, and salt. Add the chicken. Stir and cook for 5 minutes. Stir in the prepared yogurt and almond paste, and continue stir-frying for another 10 minutes. Add the water and mix well. Reduce the heat, cover, and simmer, stirring to prevent sticking, for another 10–15 minutes or until the chicken is tender. Serve garnished with the fried onions. The whole spices may be removed before serving.
Serve with naan (page 105), chapati, or paratha (pages 98–102), patta gobi aur mattar (page 68), and raita.

MURGI KA KORMA

MAKHNI MURGI

BALTI MURGI SOA WALI

STIR-FRIED CHICKEN WITH DILL

SERVES 4

8 skinless chicken thighs
1 tablespoon vegetable oil
1 tablespoon butter
1½ cups water
1 medium onion, coarsely chopped
3 large garlic cloves, minced
2 teaspoons minced fresh ginger
1 small green chili pepper, seeded and
minced (optional)
1 teaspoon paprika
1 teaspoon ground cumin
1 teaspoon garam masala (page 122)
salt, to taste
¼ cup minced fresh dill
1 large tomato, seeded and coarsely chopped

Trim any visible fat from the chicken. Wash and pat dry with paper towels. Set aside.

Heat the oil and butter in a nonstick pan over medium heat. Add the chicken thighs and fry, turning once, for 5–7 minutes or until lightly browned on both sides. Add the water and bring to a boil. Reduce the heat, cover, and simmer, stirring to prevent sticking, for 10–15 minutes or until the chicken is tender. Increase the heat to medium and stir-fry until all the liquid has evaporated.

Using a slotted spoon, remove the chicken to a plate. Return the pan to the stove over medium heat.

Add the onion, garlic, ginger, and chili pepper (if using), and stir-fry for about 2 minutes or until the onion is translucent. Stir in the spices, garam masala, salt, and dill, and continue to stir-fry for a minute longer. Reduce the heat, add the tomato and chicken, and cook over low heat for 3–4 minutes or until the chicken is heated through.

Serve with any dal dish, raita, and roti or rice.

BALTI RANGEELA MURGI

COLORFUL STIR-FRIED CHICKEN

SERVES 6

14 ounces skinless, boneless chicken breast halves
2 tablespoons vegetable oil
1 teaspoon cumin seeds
1 onion, coarsely chopped
1 tablespoon minced garlic
salt, to taste
1 teaspoon garam masala (page 122)
½ teaspoon pepper
½ teaspoon paprika
1 teaspoon ground cumin
1 small green chili pepper, seeded and
minced (optional)
1 cup coarsely sliced mushrooms
4 baby corn ears, sliced
2 medium zucchini, sliced
4 baby carrots, sliced
½ red bell pepper, seeded and cut into ¾-inch dice
½ green bell pepper, seeded and cut into ¾-inch dice

Cut the chicken into ¾-inch cubes and set aside.

Heat the oil in a wok or large nonstick pan over medium heat. Add the cumin seeds and fry for 30 seconds or until the cumin starts to crackle. Add the chicken and stir-fry for 4–5 minutes. Stir in the onion, garlic, and salt, and continue stir-frying for 3 minutes longer. Add all the remaining ingredients, except the bell peppers. Lower the heat and continue to cook, stirring, for 5–7 minutes longer or until the vegetables are almost tender. Stir in the peppers and cook for another 3 minutes. If too moist, increase the heat to medium when you add the peppers and cook until the chicken is done and the vegetables are tender but still crunchy.

As the name suggests, this is a very colorful dish. Serve with tarka dal (page 59), angoor aur akhrot raita (page 75), and roti, naan (page 105), or rice.

INDIAN FLAVOR

SHAHI KOFTA
ROYAL MEATBALLS IN GRAVY
SERVES 6 (MAKES 12 KOFTAS)

meatballs

6 dried apricots, minced
2 tablespoons minced, fresh mint leaves
2 tablespoons chopped almonds
3 tablespoons ricotta cheese
pinch of salt
1 pound ground lamb
1 teaspoon ginger paste
½ teaspoon garam masala (page 122)
½ teaspoon hot chili powder or paprika
½ teaspoon salt, or to taste

gravy

3 tablespoons vegetable oil
2 onions, minced
2 bay leaves
1 cardamom pod, cracked
1 teaspoon garlic paste
1 teaspoon ginger paste
½ teaspoon turmeric
1 teaspoon paprika
1 teaspoon garam masala
salt, to taste
2 ripe tomatoes, grated
2 tablespoons chopped cilantro
4–5 cups hot water

To make the meatballs, place the apricots, mint, almonds, cheese, and a pinch of salt in a bowl and mix well. In a separate bowl, mix together the remaining ingredients for the meatballs and divide into twelve equal portions. Grease your palm lightly and flatten one portion slightly. Place a teaspoon of the apricot mixture in the center and fold the edges in to form a small ball (*kofta*). Set aside. Repeat the process until all the meatball mixture is used up.

To make the gravy, heat the oil in a wide-based, nonstick skillet over medium heat. Add the minced onions, bay leaves, and cardamom, and stir-fry until golden brown. Stir in all the remaining gravy ingredients except for the tomatoes, cilantro, and water. Continue frying until the oil just starts to float. Add the tomatoes, 1 tablespoon of the cilantro, and 2 cups of the hot water, and bring to a boil.

Reduce the heat to low and carefully place the meatballs in the skillet in a single layer. Cover and continue cooking over low heat for 8–10 minutes. Shake the pan back and forth every minute or two to prevent sticking and to cook the meatballs evenly.

When all the water has evaporated, continue stir-frying gently for 5 minutes longer. Add the remaining water, increase the heat, and bring to a boil. Reduce the heat, cover again, and simmer for 5 minutes more. Transfer to a serving dish and garnish with the remaining cilantro.

Serve hot with gobi aloo (page 68), kachoomber raita (page 79), and chapati (page 98) or rice, or over cooked pasta with your favorite side salad.

VARIATION

Ground beef or chicken can be used instead of lamb.

KHEEMA MATTER
GROUND LAMB WITH GREEN PEAS
SERVES 6

3 tablespoons vegetable oil
2 large onions, minced in the blender
4 teaspoons garlic paste
2 teaspoons ginger paste
1 small green chili pepper, seeded and minced
2 tablespoons tomato paste
2 tablespoons chopped cilantro
1 teaspoon ground fenugreek (optional)
1 teaspoon turmeric
½ teaspoon hot chili powder
½ teaspoon paprika
1 teaspoon ground cumin
1 teaspoon ground coriander
1 teaspoon garam masala (page 122)
salt, to taste
14 ounces (1¾ cups packed) ground lamb or beef
2 large tomatoes, minced
2 cups hot water
2 cups frozen green peas
1 teaspoon chopped cilantro, to garnish

Heat the oil in a nonstick skillet over medium heat. Add the minced onions and stir-fry until golden brown. Stir in all the remaining ingredients except the last five. Continue to stir-fry until the oil just starts to float. Add the lamb or beef, chopped tomatoes, and hot water. Stir well, then cover and simmer for about 10 minutes, stirring occasionally. Add the peas, reduce the heat, and cook for another 10 minutes or until the meat is cooked and the water has evaporated. Remove the lid, stir, and cook for 5 minutes longer. Transfer to a serving dish and garnish with chopped cilantro. Serve with hot paratha (pages 101–102), sabat moong masaledar (page 61), and onion rings dressed with lemon juice and salt and pepper to taste.

PALAK GOSHT
LAMB WITH SPINACH
SERVES 6

2 onions, coarsely chopped
6–7 garlic cloves, chopped
1¼-inch piece fresh ginger, chopped
1 small green chili pepper, chopped (optional)
1 pound fresh or frozen spinach, chopped
a few sprigs of fresh dill, chopped
2 tomatoes, chopped
2 tablespoons vegetable oil
1 tablespoon unsalted butter
1 pound boneless lamb
two ¾-inch pieces cinnamon stick
½ teaspoon turmeric
2 teaspoons garam masala (page 122)
½ teaspoon hot chili powder
salt, to taste
1½–2 cups water, in batches as required

In a blender, first blend the onions, garlic, ginger, and chili pepper (if using) to a purée and remove. Then blend together the spinach and dill, and remove. Finally, blend the tomatoes to a purée and set aside.

Heat the oil and butter in a nonstick pan over medium heat. Add the lamb and cinnamon, and stir-fry for about 5 minutes. Add the onion mixture and continue to stir-fry until the lamb and onion mixture is golden brown. Add the puréed tomatoes, all the spices, and salt. Stir and cook for another 5 minutes. Stir in the spinach, cover, reduce the heat, and simmer for 15–20 minutes or until the lamb is tender, stirring to keep it from sticking. Add a little water if necessary. Palak gosht sauce should be like a thick purée.

Serve with rasedar lobia, kheera pudina raita (page 75), and chapati (page 98) or naan (page 105).

VARIATIONS
Veal, beef, or chicken can be used instead of lamb.

TIP
To reduce cooking time, I sometimes use meat tenderizer. (See label instructions for the amount.)

KHEEMA MATTER

SHAHI KORMA
LAMB IN ALMOND AND YOGURT SAUCE
SERVES 4

**Korma dishes are generally mild, with a creamy gravy.
Vegetables can be used instead of meat (see variation below).**

¼ cup plain, low-fat yogurt
¼ teaspoon cardamom seeds, pounded
1-inch piece fresh root ginger
1 tablespoon chopped garlic
3 tablespoons blanched and chopped almonds
2 tablespoons vegetable oil
1 pound boneless lamb, cut into ¾-inch cubes
2 onions, minced

2 bay leaves
4 whole cloves
½ teaspoon paprika
1½ teaspoons ground cumin
salt, to taste
½ cup cream, mixed with
 1¼ cups water
½ teaspoon garam masala (page 122)

Place the yogurt, cardamom, ginger, garlic, and almonds in a blender and blend to a smooth paste. Set aside.
In a wide-based, nonstick pan, heat the oil over medium heat. Add the lamb, onions, bay leaves, and cloves, and stir-fry for 10 minutes or until the lamb and onions have browned. Stir in the almond and yogurt paste, the paprika, ground cumin, and salt. Continue to stir and cook until all the liquid has evaporated. Stir-fry for another minute. Stir in the cream and water mixture. When it starts to boil, reduce the heat to low, cover, and simmer (stirring to prevent sticking) for 35–40 minutes longer, or until the lamb is tender and you have a thick, brown gravy. Add more liquid if too dry. Remove from the heat.

Serve hot, sprinkled with ½ teaspoon of garam masala. Include chapati (page 98), naan (page 105), or rice and kachoomber raita (page 79) in the menu.
This dish also goes well with mashed potatoes, steamed vegetables, and a side salad.

VARIATION
For a vegetarian korma, replace the meat with about 1½ pounds mixed vegetables, such as cauliflower, potatoes, beans, and carrots. Follow the same method of cooking.

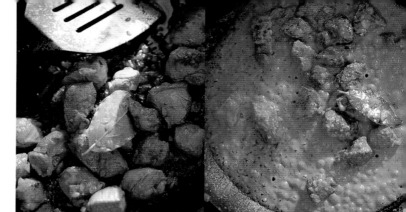

SHAHI KORMA

INDIAN FLAVOR

VINDALOO
HOT AND SOUR LAMB
SERVES 6

The amount of chili powder used can be varied according to taste. In Goa, vindaloo is made very hot. The amount of chili powder and peppercorns used in this recipe makes the dish mild in my book!

1 tablespoon cumin seeds
¼ teaspoon cardamom seeds
two ¾-inch pieces cinnamon stick
8 whole cloves
10 whole peppercorns
1 cup vinegar, preferably malt vinegar
1 teaspoon mustard powder
1 teaspoon hot chili powder, or to taste
1 teaspoon paprika
1 teaspoon turmeric
1 teaspoon granulated sugar
1¾ pounds boneless lamb, cut into 2-inch cubes
3 tablespoons vegetable oil
1 onion, minced
2 teaspoons ginger paste
1 tablespoon garlic paste
salt, to taste
3 cups hot water

Grind the cumin seeds, cardamom seeds, cinnamon, cloves, and peppercorns in a coffee grinder. Transfer to a bowl. Add the vinegar to the ground spices. Stir in the mustard, chili powder, paprika, turmeric, and sugar, and mix well. Add the lamb and mix thoroughly. Leave to marinate for 5–6 hours or preferably overnight.

Heat the oil in a nonstick pan over medium heat. Add the onion and sauté until golden brown. Stir in the ginger and garlic pastes, and stir-fry for 30 seconds. Stir in the marinated lamb and salt, and cook for 2–3 minutes. Add the water and bring to a boil. Reduce the heat to low, cover, and simmer for an hour or so, stirring now and then, or until the lamb is tender.

Best served with plain rice. My family enjoys it with crusty Italian bread, as well.

VARIATIONS
Beef or chicken can be used instead of lamb. This dish can also be cooked in the oven. Follow the instructions until after the water is added. Preheat the oven to 350°F and cook the vindaloo, covered, for 1–1½ hours or until the lamb is tender.

VEGETARIAN
DISHES

This section includes various delicious ways of cooking paneer (homemade cheese) and legumes (peas, beans, and lentils).

Cooked legumes (*dal* in Hindi), of which there are many kinds in India, generally form the nucleus of a menu plan for vegetarians, as they are a good source of protein, some B vitamins, and fiber. Proteins from this source have one or more essential amino acids missing when eaten individually. These are therefore termed incomplete proteins and are considered lesser proteins than animal proteins. Soybeans are the only exception, being equal in quality to animal protein. However, when eaten in combination with certain other foods, legumes will meet the total protein requirement of vegetarians very effectively. Since the body does not store amino acids as it does carbohydrates and fat, it is advisable, especially for growing children and vegetarians, to include these combinations in the same meal to ensure the availability of all the essential amino acids. Legumes should be combined with any of the following: grains, nuts and seeds, or milk products.

A typical Indian meal is an excellent example of the correct combination for a nutritionally balanced meal, which is why Indian food provides such an attractive option for vegetarians. Rice or wheat roti (grains) are combined with a legume and yogurt, buttermilk, or other milk product and a vegetable at each meal.

A great variety of legumes is grown in India, and there are many different ways of cooking them with meat and vegetables. The recipes that follow provide interesting ways of adding variety to your daily food plan. To make things simpler, I have provided recipes using only those legumes that I have seen on supermarket shelves. For convenience I have used canned legumes in place of the dried variety, as this eliminates soaking and cooking time.

Cooking times of the dry product vary according to the type of legume used, and whole legumes take longer to cook than the split variety. I generally use a pressure cooker to cut down on cooking time. I also soak green mung beans in warm water for 2–3 hours or preferably overnight. As a general rule, any cooked dal should not be too watery, but should have a fairly mushy consistency. For tempering or seasoning we use ghee, which is available from many large supermarkets or Indian markets. I have used half oil and half butter in some recipes. Feel free to substitute oil for butter.

Most of the dishes presented here can be frozen for several weeks without any loss of flavor.

MATTAR PANEER

HOMEMADE CHEESE WITH GREEN PEAS

SERVES 6

A very nutritious vegetarian dish.

12 ounces low-fat paneer (page 119)
3 tablespoons vegetable oil
2 onions, minced
1 teaspoon garlic paste
2 teaspoons ginger paste
1 teaspoon turmeric
2 teaspoons ground cumin
2 teaspoons ground coriander
1 teaspoon paprika
½ teaspoon hot chili powder (optional)
1 teaspoon garam masala (page 122)
2 large tomatoes, grated
2 tablespoons minced cilantro
2 cups frozen green peas
salt, to taste
3 cups hot water
1 teaspoon chopped cilantro, to garnish

Cut the paneer into ¾-inch cubes and set aside. Heat the oil in a nonstick pan over medium heat. Add the onions and stir-fry until golden brown. Stir in the garlic and ginger pastes and fry for another 30 seconds. Add all the dry spices and tomatoes and continue to stir-fry until some oil starts to separate. Stir in the minced cilantro, the peas, salt, and paneer. Stir-fry for another minute, then add the water. Bring to a boil, cover, and cook for 5 minutes or until the peas are tender and you have a thick, aromatic sauce. Remove from the heat and transfer to a serving bowl. Sprinkle with the chopped cilantro.
Serve hot with aloo soya tikki (page 17), pudina chutney (page 123), and chapati (page 98), paratha (pages 101–102), or rice.

BALTI PANEER

STIR-FRIED HOMEMADE CHEESE

SERVES 6

1 tablespoon coriander seeds
2 teaspoons cumin seeds
½ teaspoon whole peppercorns
½ teaspoon fenugreek seeds*
2 tablespoons vegetable oil
1 tablespoon unsalted butter
2 onions, minced
2 teaspoons minced garlic
1 teaspoon garam masala (page 122)
½ teaspoon hot chili powder (optional)
½ teaspoon paprika
salt, to taste
2 tomatoes, chopped
½ red bell pepper, julienned
½ green bell pepper, julienned
1 pound low-fat paneer (page 119), cut into ¾-inch cubes

Place the coriander, cumin, peppercorns, and fenugreek seeds in a coffee grinder or blender and grind coarsely by pulsing the machine on and off, or use a mortar and pestle. Set aside.
Heat the oil and butter in a wok or any other round-bottomed pan over medium heat. Add the onions and garlic and sauté until the onions just start to turn golden. Add the pounded spices along with the other spices and salt. Stir-fry for 30 seconds, then stir in the tomatoes and peppers. Continue to stir and cook until the peppers are tender but still crunchy. Stir in the paneer, lower the heat, and stir-fry for about 5–7 minutes or until the paneer is heated through. Remove from the heat.
Serve with masoor dal sabzi wali (page 59), kachoomber raita (page 79), paratha (pages 101–102), and onion rings dressed with lemon juice and salt and pepper to taste.

* Though important for the right flavor, omit if not available.

MATTAR PANEER

BALTI PANEER

SOYA MATTAR
SOY PROTEIN WITH GREEN PEAS
SERVES 6

1½ cups TVP granules
1 tablespoon cumin seeds
1 tablespoon coriander seeds
6 whole cloves
¼ teaspoon cardamom seeds
¾-inch piece cinnamon stick, broken into small bits
½ teaspoon fennel seeds
2 tablespoons vegetable oil
1 tablespoon unsalted butter
2 large onions, minced
4 teaspoons garlic paste

2 teaspoons minced fresh ginger
1 small green chili pepper, seeded and chopped (optional)
½ teaspoon turmeric
1 teaspoon paprika
salt, to taste
3 tablespoons tomato paste
2 tomatoes, grated
1 teaspoon garam masala (page 122)
2 cups hot water
3 cups green peas
2 tablespoons minced cilantro

Prepare the TVP (see page 120). Set aside. Dry-fry all the whole spices in a frying pan over low heat until brown and aromatic. Cool and grind to a powder in a coffee grinder. Set aside.

Heat the oil and butter in a nonstick pan over medium heat. Add the onions and sauté until light golden in color. Stir in the garlic, ginger, and chili pepper (if using). Sauté for a minute longer. Stir in the browned spices, the other dry spices, salt, tomato paste, grated tomatoes, and garam masala, and cook, stirring, for 5 minutes or until oil starts to surface. Add the prepared TVP and stir-fry for 3–4 minutes. Add the water, stir, and bring to a boil. Reduce the heat and cook, covered, stirring occasionally, for 10–15 minutes or until little liquid remains. Add the peas and cook for another 5–7 minutes or until the peas are cooked and no liquid remains. Add the cilantro and cook, stirring, for another 5 minutes. Remove from the heat.

Since this is a dry dish, serve it with sabat moong masaledar (page 61) or sabat masoor (page 65), angoor aur akhrot raita (page 75), and chapati (page 98), naan (page 105), or rice.

SOYA KORMA

SOY PROTEIN WITH CREAMY GRAVY

SERVES 6

Soy korma is rich in protein, calcium, vitamins, and fiber, and should be included in your meal plan often, especially if you are a vegetarian.

¾ cup TVP granules
1 tablespoon poppy seeds
2 teaspoons sesame seeds
6 garlic cloves
2 teaspoons chopped fresh ginger
¾ cup plain low-fat or homemade yogurt
2 teaspoons garam masala (page 122)
1 teaspoon ground coriander
2 teaspoons ground cumin
½ teaspoon hot chili powder, or to taste
½ teaspoon paprika
½ teaspoon pepper
salt, to taste
2 tablespoons vegetable oil

1 tablespoon unsalted butter
3 cardamom pods, cracked
2 bay leaves
¼-inch piece cinnamon stick
2 onions, minced or grated
8 baby potatoes, peeled
1½ cups hot water (or more if needed)
1 cup frozen green peas
¼ cup tomato paste
1 tablespoon lemon juice
¼ cup cream
2 teaspoons minced cilantro
1 teaspoon minced fresh mint leaves, for garnish

Prepare the TVP (see page 120). Set aside. Dry-fry the poppy and sesame seeds in a small frying pan over low heat until light golden in color. Let cool for a minute or so. Place the seeds in a blender along with the garlic and ginger, and blend until a smooth paste is formed. If it is too dry to blend, add a little water. Transfer to a small bowl and set aside.

Combine the yogurt, all the dry spices, and salt in a bowl and whisk until smooth. Place the oil and butter in a wide-based nonstick pan and heat over medium heat. Add the cardamom, bay leaves, and cinnamon, and fry for 30 seconds. Stir in the onions and sauté until golden brown. Add the seed paste and stir-fry for 30–40 seconds. Add the prepared TVP and cook, stirring, for another minute. Stir in the yogurt mixture, potatoes, and water, and bring to a boil, stirring continuously. Reduce the heat to low, cover, and cook, stirring occasionally, for 12–15 minutes or until the potatoes are cooked.

Stir in all the remaining ingredients except for the mint. If it is too dry, add some more hot water to get the desired consistency. Stir and cook for 2–3 minutes longer or until the korma starts to simmer again. Remove from the heat. Transfer to a serving dish and garnish with the mint.

Serve hot with any side vegetable dish and yogurt dish, along with chapati (page 98) or rolls.

MASOOR DAL SABZI WALI

TARKA DAL
SEASONED LENTILS
SERVES 4–5

2½ cups water (or more if required)
1 teaspoon salt, or to taste
1 cup red lentils, picked over and rinsed
1 small garlic clove, chopped and crushed
½ teaspoon turmeric
seasoning
1 tablespoon vegetable oil
1 tablespoon butter
1 small onion, minced
1 teaspoon cumin seeds
1 small green chili pepper, seeded and
chopped (optional)
1 tablespoon minced cilantro
½ teaspoon paprika
2 medium tomatoes, minced

In a pan, bring the water to a boil over medium heat. Add the salt, lentils, garlic, and turmeric, stir, and bring to a boil again. Reduce the heat, cover partially, and cook for 25–30 minutes, until the lentils are soft and mushy, stirring occasionally. Remove from the heat and prepare the seasoning.
Heat the oil and butter in a small frying pan over medium heat. Add the onion, cumin seeds, and chili pepper (if using), and sauté for 5 minutes or until the onion turns golden brown. Stir in all the remaining ingredients and cook, stirring, for 4–5 minutes longer or until the tomatoes are soft. Remove from the heat and add to the cooked lentils. Stir and cover tightly. Let stand for 5 minutes before serving to allow the flavors to merge.
Serve with plain rice or biryani, vegetable pulao or roti, and any vegetable or meat dish.

TIP
Can be prepared in advance and reheated just before serving.

MASOOR DAL SABZI WALI
RED LENTILS WITH VEGETABLES
SERVES 6

4 cups water
1 cup red lentils, picked over and rinsed
1 teaspoon garlic paste
1 teaspoon turmeric
salt, to taste
1 cup thinly sliced carrots
1 cup sliced zucchini
1 cup broccoli florets
1 medium potato, peeled and cut into ¾-inch cubes
seasoning
1 tablespoon vegetable oil
1 tablespoon butter
1 medium onion, minced
2 teaspoons ground cumin
2 teaspoons ground coriander
½ teaspoon hot chili powder
½ teaspoon paprika
2 tomatoes, chopped
1 tablespoon minced cilantro

In a pan, bring the water to a boil over medium heat. Add the lentils, garlic, turmeric, and salt. Reduce the heat, cover partially, and simmer for 15–20 minutes or until the lentils are almost cooked. Stir in all the vegetables, cover, and continue cooking for another 10–15 minutes or until the vegetables are tender but still crunchy. Remove from the heat and keep warm.
Heat the oil and butter in a small frying pan over medium heat. Add the onion and sauté until golden brown. Add all the dry spices and tomatoes. Stir-fry for about 3–5 minutes or until the tomatoes are soft. Stir in the minced cilantro. Remove from the heat and add to the cooked lentils and vegetables. Stir and cover tightly. Let stand for 5 minutes before serving to allow the flavors to merge.
Serve with plain rice or roti, any meat dish, and a yogurt side dish for a well-balanced meal, or with any tandoori preparation and naan (page 105).

SABAT MOONG MASALEDAR

SPICY GREEN MUNG BEANS

SERVES 6

1½ cups green mung beans, picked over and soaked
overnight in water to cover
7 cups water (or more if required)
1 teaspoon ginger paste
2 teaspoons garlic paste
½ teaspoon turmeric
½ teaspoon hot chili powder
salt, to taste
seasoning
1 tablespoon vegetable oil
1 tablespoon unsalted butter
1 onion, minced
½ small green chili pepper, seeded and chopped
2 teaspoons ground cumin
2 teaspoons ground coriander
1 tomato, minced

Drain the mung beans and set aside.

In a pan, bring the water to a boil over medium heat. Add the mung beans, ginger and garlic pastes, turmeric, chili powder, and salt, stir, and bring to a boil again. Reduce the heat, cover partially, and simmer for 45–60 minutes or until the beans are cooked and mushy, stirring occasionally.

While the beans are cooking, prepare the seasoning. Heat the oil and butter in a small frying pan over medium heat. Add the onion and sauté until golden brown. Add all the dry spices and tomato. Stir and cook for 3–5 minutes or until the tomato is soft and a little oil starts to float. Remove from the heat and add to the cooked beans. Stir and cover tightly. Let stand for 5 minutes before serving to allow the flavors to merge.

Best served with any dry main dish or tandoori dish, a side vegetable of your choice, and chapati (page 98) or plain rice.

VARIATION

The mung beans can be replaced by green or brown lentils.

SHAHI DAL
ROYAL YELLOW SPLIT PEAS
SERVES 4

1 cup yellow split peas
4 cups water
salt, to taste
½ teaspoon turmeric
½ teaspoon hot chili powder
1 tablespoon unsalted butter
1 teaspoon garlic paste
¼ cup cream
1 cup plain, low-fat yogurt, whipped
seasoning
2 tablespoons unsalted butter
1 onion, minced
2 teaspoons minced garlic
½ teaspoon cumin seeds
1 teaspoon ground cumin
½ teaspoon white pepper
½ teaspoon paprika

Pick over and rinse the split peas. Drain and set aside.
In a pan, bring the water to a boil over medium heat.
Add the split peas, salt, turmeric, chili powder,
butter, and garlic paste. Stir and bring to a boil again.
Reduce the heat, cover partially, and simmer for
20–25 minutes, stirring occasionally, or until
the split peas are cooked but not mushy.
Stir in the cream and then the yogurt. Continue to
cook, stirring, for another 10 minutes.
Remove from the heat.
To make the seasoning, heat the butter in
a small frying pan over medium heat. Add the onion,
garlic, and cumin seeds, and sauté until the onion
is golden brown. Add the remaining ingredients,
remove from the heat immediately, and add to the
cooked split peas.
Makes an excellent meal when served with
gobi aloo (page 68), raita, and chapati (page 98).

CHOLE AUR KHUMB
CHICKPEAS WITH MUSHROOMS
SERVES 6

14-ounce can chickpeas (garbanzo beans)
7 ounces fresh button mushrooms
3 tablespoons vegetable oil
2 onions, minced or grated
1 tablespoon garlic paste
2 teaspoons ginger paste
3 tablespoons tomato paste
3 tomatoes, grated
½ teaspoon turmeric
½ teaspoon hot chili powder
½ teaspoon paprika
2 teaspoons ground cumin
2 teaspoons garam masala (page 122)
salt, to taste
2 cups hot water
2 teaspoons chopped cilantro, to garnish

Drain the chickpeas, then rinse and drain again.
Set aside.
Wash the mushrooms and cut vertically into two
or four pieces, depending on the size. Set aside.
Heat the oil in a nonstick pan over medium heat.
Stir in the onions and sauté until brown. Add the
garlic and ginger pastes and stir-fry for 30 seconds.
Add the tomato paste and grated tomatoes.
Continue to stir and cook for 5 minutes or until the
oil just starts to float. Stir in all the spices and salt,
and stir well to mix. Add the mushrooms and sauté
for 5 minutes, stirring. Add the chickpeas and stir to
combine. Add the water and bring to a boil. Reduce
the heat and simmer, covered, for 5 minutes.
Remove from the heat, transfer to a serving bowl,
and garnish with cilantro.
Serve with any vegetable side dish, a yogurt
dish, and chapati (page 98) or rice for a perfect
vegetable/protein combination, or with any
tandoori preparation.

SHAHI DAL

CHOLE AUR KHUMB

SABAT MASOOR

SPICY BROWN LENTILS

SERVES 4

14-ounce can brown lentils
2 tablespoons vegetable oil
1 onion, minced or grated
2 teaspoons garlic paste
½ teaspoon ginger paste
½ teaspoon turmeric
1 teaspoon paprika
1 teaspoon ground cumin
1 teaspoon ground coriander
½ teaspoon garam masala (page 122)
½ small green chili pepper, chopped (optional)
1 large tomato, grated
2 tablespoons minced cilantro
salt, to taste
2 cups hot water
1 teaspoon chopped cilantro, to garnish

Drain the lentils, rinse with fresh water, drain again, and set aside.

In a deep pan, heat the oil over medium heat. Add the onion and sauté until golden brown. Lower the heat. Add the garlic and ginger pastes, and stir-fry for 30 seconds. Stir in all the dry spices, the chili pepper (if using), tomato, minced cilantro, and salt. Stir and cook for 2–3 minutes or until the oil just starts to float. Add the lentils and water, and bring to a boil. Reduce the heat, cover, and simmer for 10 minutes. Remove from the heat and mash the lentils with the back of a spoon against the side of the pan to get a mushy texture. Transfer to a serving dish and garnish with the chopped cilantro.

Serve hot with any nonvegetarian main dish or tandoori preparation, or a side dish of vegetables, chapati (page 98) or rolls, and plain yogurt or raita (pages 75–79).

SIDE DISHES

YOGURT AND VEGETABLE

Nutrition experts around the world are in agreement that our daily food plan should include plenty of fresh vegetables. Apart from being an excellent source of vitamins, minerals, and fiber, and low in calories, they add color, flavor, and texture to our menu. Since the majority of the Indian population is vegetarian, there is a wonderful variety of delicious vegetable side dishes in Indian cuisine. Vegetables are cooked either with gravy or dry, and in different combinations, using different herbs and spices.

A common fault in Indian cooking seems to be a tendency to overcook vegetables, although this is changing as people become more aware of the loss of important nutrients that results from overcooking. Cooked vegetables should not be kept hot after cooking, as this will also destroy heat-sensitive nutrients. Instead, reheat in the microwave or on top of the stove just before serving. Raw vegetables are used in salads or added to yogurt to make raita.

I have selected recipes using vegetables that should be very familiar, readily available, and easy to cook.

Apart from the extensive use of yogurt in cooking, no Indian meal is complete without a yogurt side dish, either in the form of raita—yogurt mixed with vegetables—or on its own. It provides a cooling contrast to spicy dishes and is a good source of calcium and protein.

I have used low-fat yogurt in the recipes that follow, but feel free to substitute whole-milk yogurt or your own homemade yogurt (page 118). Raita goes particularly well with rice pulao or biryani.

GOBI ALOO
CAULIFLOWER WITH POTATOES
SERVES 4

1 tablespoon vegetable oil
1 teaspoon cumin seeds
1 teaspoon minced garlic
1 teaspoon minced fresh ginger
½ teaspoon turmeric
½ teaspoon paprika

1 teaspoon ground cumin
½ teaspoon garam masala (page 122)
salt, to taste
2 medium potatoes, peeled and cut into small pieces
1 pound cauliflower, cut into small florets
1 tablespoon chopped cilantro

Heat the oil in a wide-based, nonstick pan over medium heat. Stir in the cumin seeds, garlic, and ginger, and fry for a minute or until the garlic just starts to change color. Reduce the heat to low and add all the spices, salt, and potatoes. Cook, covered, for 5–7 minutes, stirring occasionally. Add the cauliflower and cilantro, reduce the heat to very low, cover, and cook, stirring the vegetables to keep them from sticking and burning, until tender.

Serve with any meat or vegetarian main dish, chapati (page 98) or paratha (pages 101–102), and raita (pages 75–79) or plain yogurt.

TIP
You can add a bit of water to keep the vegetables from sticking.

PATTA GOBI AUR MATTAR
CABBAGE WITH PEAS
SERVES 4

4 teaspoons vegetable oil
1 teaspoon cumin seeds
14 ounces (about 6 cups) cabbage, shredded
1 tomato, chopped
½ teaspoon turmeric

½ teaspoon garam masala (page 122)
½ teaspoon paprika
salt, to taste
1½ cups frozen green peas, thawed

Heat the oil in a wide-based pan over medium heat. Add the cumin seeds and fry for a few seconds or until the cumin starts to change color. Stir in the cabbage, tomato, spices, and salt. Stir and cook for 5 minutes.

Add the peas and continue to stir-fry for 5 minutes longer or until the cabbage is tender but crunchy and dry. Remove from the heat.

Serve with any meat or vegetarian main dish, chapati (page 98) or paratha (pages 101–102), and raita (pages 75–79) or plain yogurt.

SABZI AUR CHANNE

SABZI AUR CHANNE
MIXED VEGETABLES WITH CHICKPEAS
SERVES 6–8

2 tablespoons tomato paste
1 cup plain, low-fat yogurt
½ teaspoon hot chili powder
1 teaspoon paprika
1 teaspoon garam masala
¼ teaspoon pepper
¼ teaspoon ground mace
1 teaspoon ginger paste
½ teaspoon salt
14-ounce can chickpeas (garbanzo beans)
2 tablespoons vegetable oil
1 tablespoon unsalted butter
1¼-inch piece cinnamon stick
2 cardamom pods, cracked
2 bay leaves
2 onions, coarsely chopped
1 teaspoon garlic paste
1 potato, peeled and cut into ¾-inch cubes
2 cups small cauliflower florets
10 green beans, cut into ¾-inch pieces
2 zucchini, sliced
1 tablespoon minced cilantro
½ cup hot water, or more if required
salt, to taste
¼ cup cream
2 teaspoons sesame seeds, toasted, to garnish

Place the tomato paste, yogurt, all the dry ground spices, ginger paste, and ½ teaspoon salt in a mixing bowl and whisk until smooth. Set aside.

Drain and rinse the chickpeas, and drain again. Set aside.

Heat the oil and butter in a wok or a deep pan over medium heat. Stir in the cinnamon, cardamom, bay leaves, onions, and garlic paste, and stir-fry until the onion is golden brown. Stir in the yogurt mixture and continue to stir and cook until the mixture starts to bubble. Reduce the heat to low, cover, and simmer for 3–4 minutes. Add all the vegetables, the cilantro, water, and salt. Mix, then cover and cook until the vegetables are tender but still crunchy. Stir in the cream and bring the mixture to a boil. Remove from the heat, transfer to a serving dish, and sprinkle with sesame seeds to garnish.

Serve with any meat or vegetarian main dish, rice, and raita (pages 75–79) or plain yogurt.

PALAK DAL

INDIAN FLAVOR

PALAK DAL
SPINACH AND SPLIT PEAS
SERVES 4

¼ cup yellow split peas
2 cups water
½ teaspoon salt
2 tablespoons vegetable oil
1 onion, minced
2 teaspoons minced garlic
½ teaspoon ginger paste
1 teaspoon ground cumin
1 teaspoon paprika
1 teaspoon ground coriander
salt, to taste
1 pound spinach, minced
1 tablespoon lemon juice

Pick over and rinse the split peas. In a small saucepan, bring the water to a boil. Add ½ teaspoon salt and the split peas. Lower the heat and simmer until the peas are soft but not mushy. Remove from the heat and drain. Set aside.
Heat the oil in a wide-based pan over medium heat. Add the onion, garlic, and ginger, and sauté for 2 minutes or until the onion is translucent. Add all the spices, salt, the spinach, and lemon juice, and mix well.
Cook, uncovered, for 2 minutes or until the spinach has wilted and the juices have been released. Continue to cook and stir for 5–7 minutes longer or until the spinach is cooked and all excess liquid has evaporated. Stir in the cooked split peas, mix well, and cook for another minute.
Serve with any meat or vegetarian main dish, chapati (page 98) or paratha (pages 101–102), and raita (pages 75–79) or plain yogurt.

VEGETABLE JALFREZI
MIXED VEGETABLES
SERVES 6–8

Although lentils are not traditionally part of this vegetable dish, I like to use them to enhance the nutritive value, as well as the flavor and texture.

2 tablespoons vegetable oil
1 teaspoon cumin seeds
2 onions, coarsely chopped
1 teaspoon dried red pepper flakes, or to taste
1½ cups seeded and coarsely chopped green or red bell pepper (or both)
3 cups coarsely chopped cabbage
1 cup coarsely chopped green beans
1 cup sliced carrots
1 teaspoon ginger paste
2 teaspoons minced fresh ginger
½ teaspoon pepper
14-ounce can whole lentils, rinsed and drained
½ teaspoon paprika
1 teaspoon ground cumin
salt, to taste
2 tablespoons chopped cilantro
5 tablespoons tomato paste
1½ tablespoons white vinegar

Heat the oil in a wide-based pan over medium heat. Add the cumin seeds, onions, and pepper flakes, and sauté for a minute. Stir in all the remaining ingredients, except the tomato paste and vinegar. Reduce the heat, cover, and cook for about 10 minutes or until the vegetables are just tender. Stir in the tomato paste and vinegar, mix well, and cook for 2 minutes longer. Remove from the heat and transfer to a serving dish.
Serve hot with any meat dish, aloo soya tikki (page 17), or balti paneer (page 52), along with chapati (page 98) or paratha (pages 101–102).

MASALA BHINDI AUR DAL

SPICY OKRA WITH YELLOW LENTILS

SERVES 4

¾ cup yellow lentils or yellow split peas
3 cups water
½ teaspoon salt
2 tablespoons vegetable oil
1 teaspoon cumin seeds, coarsely ground
1 teaspoon coriander seeds, coarsely ground
1 large onion, thinly sliced
2 teaspoons garlic paste
1 teaspoon ginger paste
½ teaspoon turmeric
½ teaspoon hot chili powder, or to taste
2 teaspoons ground coriander
salt, to taste
2 teaspoons raw mango powder,
or 1 tablespoon lemon juice
14 ounces okra, cut into ½-inch pieces
1 large tomato, coarsely chopped

Pick over and rinse the lentils or split peas. Place the water and salt in a saucepan and bring to a boil over medium heat. Add the lentils and cook until soft but not mushy. Drain and set aside.
Heat the oil in a wok or any round-bottomed pan over medium heat. Stir in the ground cumin and coriander seeds and fry for 30 seconds. Add the onion and sauté until golden brown in color. Stir in all the remaining ingredients, except the cooked lentils and tomato. Stir and cook for 5 minutes or until the okra is almost tender. Stir in the cooked lentils and tomatoes, and cook for 2 minutes longer. Remove from the heat. Transfer to a serving dish. Serve hot with any meat dish or vegetarian main dish, plus chapati (page 98) and yogurt raita (pages 75–79), or with plain rice and pudina chutney (page 123).

SABAT SABZIAN (BALTI-STYLE)

STIR-FRIED BABY VEGETABLES

SERVES 6 AS A SIDE DISH OR 4 AS A MAIN DISH

2 tablespoons vegetable oil
4 small onions or shallots, peeled and halved
1 teaspoon garlic paste
1 teaspoon ginger paste
½ teaspoon hot chili powder, or to taste
½ teaspoon paprika
1 teaspoon ground cumin
½ teaspoon garam masala (page 122)
¼ cup tomato paste
8 small zucchini
8 baby carrots
8 baby corn ears
½ cup water
8 baby potatoes, cooked and peeled
14-ounce can chickpeas (garbanzo beans), rinsed
and drained
8 cherry tomatoes
salt, to taste
4 teaspoons sesame seeds

Heat the oil in a wok or deep, round-bottomed pan over medium heat. Add the onions or shallots, and the garlic and ginger pastes, and stir-fry for about a minute. Add all the dry spices and tomato paste, and cook, stirring, for another minute. Stir in the zucchini, carrots, corn, and water. Cover and cook for 8–10 minutes or until the vegetables are tender but still crunchy. Stir in the potatoes, chickpeas, tomatoes, salt, and 2 teaspoons sesame seeds. Stir-fry for 2 minutes or until the potatoes are heated through. Remove from the heat. Transfer to a serving dish and sprinkle with the remaining sesame seeds.
Serve hot with any meat dish or vegetarian main dish, chapati (page 98) or rice, and homemade yogurt (page 118), or serve as a main dish along with salad and bread for a healthy vegetarian meal.

VARIATION
Any combination of vegetables can be used in place of those suggested above.

BAINGAN BHARTHA
ROASTED EGGPLANT WITH HERBS AND ONIONS
SERVES 6

2 large, firm eggplants
1 tablespoon vegetable oil
1 tablespoon unsalted butter
1 medium onion, chopped
1 teaspoon minced fresh ginger
2 tomatoes, minced
1 cup frozen green peas, thawed
2 tablespoons chopped cilantro
½ teaspoon paprika
½ small green chili pepper, seeded and chopped (optional)
salt, to taste

Smear the eggplants with a little oil and roast them under a hot broiler until they are soft and the outer skin is wrinkled and charred. Place under running water and peel off the skin. Remove the stems and mash the eggplant flesh with a potato masher or fork into a smooth, paste-like consistency. Set aside.

Heat the oil and butter in a frying pan over medium heat. Add the onion and ginger. Sauté for a minute, then stir in all the remaining ingredients, except the eggplant paste. Stir-fry for 2 minutes. Add the eggplant and continue to stir-fry for another 2 minutes. Remove from the heat and transfer to a serving dish.

Serve hot with any meat dish or vegetarian main dish, paratha (pages 101–102), and yogurt raita (pages 75–79) or plain yogurt.

ANGOOR AUR AKHROT RAITA
YOGURT WITH GRAPES AND WALNUTS
SERVES 4

2 cups plain, low-fat yogurt
½ teaspoon ground cumin
½ teaspoon pepper
½ teaspoon hot chili powder (optional)
1 teaspoon sugar
salt, to taste
¾ cup seedless grapes, cut in half
¼ cup coarsely chopped walnuts
pinch of hot chili powder, to garnish

Beat the yogurt, spices, sugar, and salt in a bowl with a fork or whisk until smooth and creamy. Add the grapes and walnuts, saving 1 teaspoon of walnuts to garnish. Mix well, then sprinkle with a pinch of chili powder and the remaining walnuts. Serve chilled.

KHEERA PUDINA RAITA
YOGURT WITH CUCUMBER AND MINT
SERVES 4

2 cups plain, low-fat yogurt
½ teaspoon toasted ground cumin (page 122)
½ teaspoon ground cumin
¼ teaspoon hot chili powder
1 small green chili pepper, seeded and
  minced (optional)
¼ teaspoon pepper
1 teaspoon sugar
salt, to taste
¾ cup peeled and grated cucumber
1½ tablespoons chopped, fresh mint leaves
pinch each of toasted ground cumin and hot chili
  powder, to garnish

Beat the yogurt, spices, sugar, and salt in a bowl until smooth and creamy. Stir in the cucumber and mint, saving some mint. Sprinkle with a pinch each of toasted ground cumin and chili powder and the remaining mint. Serve chilled.

BAINGAN KA RAITA
YOGURT WITH EGGPLANT
SERVES 4

1 small eggplant
2 cups plain, low-fat yogurt
1 teaspoon ground coriander
½ teaspoon pepper
½ teaspoon paprika
salt, to taste
2 small green onions, minced, with green tops
1 tablespoon minced cilantro
a little hot chili powder, to garnish

Roast the whole eggplant under a preheated broiler until soft and the skin is charred—almost black. Cool under running cold water, then peel off the skin. Mash the pulp into a fine paste. Set aside. Place the yogurt, spices, and salt in a bowl. Beat until smooth and creamy.
Stir in the eggplant pulp, green onions, and cilantro. Mix thoroughly. Serve chilled, sprinkled with a little chili powder.

PALAK RAITA
YOGURT WITH SPINACH
SERVES 4

sprinkling of water
¼ teaspoon salt
1½ cups minced spinach, washed
2 cups plain, low-fat yogurt
1 teaspoon minced fresh dill
½ teaspoon ginger paste
½ teaspoon toasted ground cumin (page 122)
1 teaspoon ground cumin
2 teaspoons granulated sugar
salt, to taste
a little hot chili powder, to garnish
a little toasted ground cumin, to garnish

Place a small pan over medium heat and add a bit of water and ¼ teaspoon of salt. Add the spinach and stir well. Cook for a minute or until the spinach has wilted. Increase the heat and continue cooking, uncovered, until the water has evaporated. Remove from the heat and allow to cool.
   Place the remaining ingredients, except the garnishes, in a bowl and beat until smooth and creamy. Add the spinach and mix thoroughly. Serve chilled, sprinkled with a little chili powder and toasted ground cumin.

PALAK RAITA

BAINGAN KA RAITA

KACHOOMBER RAITA
MIXED VEGETABLES IN YOGURT
SERVES 4

2 cups plain, low-fat yogurt
½ teaspoon toasted ground cumin (page 122)
1 teaspoon ground cumin
½ teaspoon pepper
½ teaspoon paprika
1 teaspoon grated lemon rind
¼ cup minced cucumber
¼ cup chopped tomato
1 cup chopped, crisp lettuce
1 tablespoon minced onion
1 tablespoon minced, fresh mint leaves
salt, to taste
paprika or toasted ground cumin, to garnish

Place the yogurt, all the spices, and the lemon rind in a bowl and whisk to mix. Stir in all the vegetables and salt. Garnish with a little paprika or toasted ground cumin. Serve chilled.

VARIATION
Replace the cucumber, tomato, and lettuce with 1½ cups finely diced, cooked potato and you have a delicious aloo (potato) raita, slightly different from the recipe below.

ALOO RAITA
YOGURT WITH POTATOES
SERVES 4

2 cups plain, low-fat yogurt
½ teaspoon toasted ground cumin (page 122)
½ teaspoon ground cumin
½ teaspoon pepper
salt, to taste
1 tablespoon minced fresh mint leaves
2 tablespoons minced green onion
2 medium potatoes, cut into small pieces
1 small green chili pepper, seeded and minced (optional)
paprika or hot chili powder, to garnish

Place the yogurt, cumin, pepper, salt, and mint in a mixing bowl and whisk together. Stir in all the remaining ingredients except the garnish. Adjust the seasoning, if needed. Transfer to a serving bowl and garnish with a dusting of paprika or chili powder. Serve chilled.

ALOO RAITA **(TOP)** AND
KACHOOMBER RAITA **(BOTTOM)**

No Indian meal is considered complete without either rice or bread (chapati, roti, or naan) on the menu. In northern India, wheat forms the basis of the meal, while in the south, rice is more common. From a nutritional point of view, rice and grains should form the major part of our diet, providing about sixty percent of our total daily calories to provide us with the energy necessary for important bodily functions.

There are different varieties of rice available in India, and different types suit different dishes. The best variety available, and the most highly regarded, is basmati, which is mainly used for pulao and biryani. It has long, slender grains and a fragrant aroma. Round, short-grained rice and parboiled rice are more commonly used.

The quality of any rice improves with age—especially basmati. Freshly harvested rice becomes starchy and, when cooked, does not increase in volume as much as rice that has been stored for a year or more. The aroma and flavor also improve with age and storage.

fore cooking rice, always rinse it gently but thoroughly in a colander or

under running water until the water runs clear. This removes starch

cles and improves the texture of the cooked rice. To half-cook rice, for

recipes that require it, test by pressing a grain or two between your thumb

index finger—the rice should be soft on top and hard in the middle.

e most popular rice preparations are plain boiled, pulao, and biryani.

RICE
DISHES

BOILED RICE

The rice is simply cooked in lightly salted, boiling water. When it is cooked, it is drained and served with cooked legumes, or with fish, meat, or vegetable dishes. Southern Indians generally serve boiled rice at every meal, whereas northern Indians will serve it only with certain dishes—for example, with punjabi rajma.

RICE PULAO

Pulao was introduced to India by the Moguls, and today it is more popular in the northern parts of India than in the south. It is basically a combination of rice with meat, chicken, vegetables, or legumes, with various spices, cooked in a tightly covered pan over low heat with just enough water to be absorbed by the rice. Different types of pulao are prepared for festive occasions and holidays.

Only the best-quality rice should be used for preparing pulao. It can be served as a main dish along with raita (a yogurt side dish) and chutney. Vegetable pulao goes very well with roast lamb, grilled pork, or steak.

Pulao freezes well and can be reheated in the microwave before serving. It will keep fresh for 2–3 days in the refrigerator.

SABZI KI BIRYANI

BIRYANI

Like pulao, biryani was brought to India by the Moguls. It is a very attractive, elegant dish prepared for special occasions. Though usually cooked with meat, chicken, or fish, the vegetarian version uses cauliflower, beans, carrots, peas, nuts, and fruits, and is equally wonderful.

The cooking method is different from that of pulao and is more time-consuming. Partially cooked rice and meat or vegetables are layered in a heavy, flat-bottomed pan and then cooked. Traditionally, biryani should be cooked over a very low heat in a pot with a tight lid that is sealed with a flour dough to contain the steam and aromas. I use an easier method, however. After layering, I cover the pot first with foil and then place the lid on tightly. It can either be cooked on top of the stove or baked in the oven after layering.

One of the most important ingredients used in biryani is saffron soaked in warm milk, which is drizzled over the rice at the time of layering. Saffron turns some of the rice grains an orange color and also gives a very distinctive aroma to biryani. Though used in tiny amounts, saffron is a very expensive spice, so you may prefer to omit it. As a substitute, a little yellow food coloring diluted with some water will serve the purpose, although the delicate flavor of saffron will be missing.

I have used basmati rice in my recipes, which is easily available under various brand names. If it is not available, use any good-quality, long-grain rice instead.

Do not be put off by the long list of ingredients for biryani and what seems to be a laborious method of cooking. Once you have assembled all the ingredients and read the recipe carefully, you will really enjoy making it, and the joy of eating it with your family or friends will make your effort more than worthwhile.

Always use a heavy-bottomed, flat pan for preparing recipes in this section.

MATTAR PULAO

KHUMB WALA PULAO

MATTAR PULAO
RICE WITH GREEN PEAS
SERVES 4

4 teaspoons vegetable oil
2 bay leaves
2 cardamom pods, cracked
1 medium onion, thinly sliced
½ teaspoon cumin seeds
2¾ cups water
1½ cups frozen green peas, thawed
1½ cups basmati rice, rinsed and drained
1½ teaspoons salt, or to taste

Heat the oil in a pan over medium heat. Stir in the bay leaves and cardamom and fry for 30 seconds. Add the onion and cumin seeds and stir-fry until golden brown. Add the water, bring to a boil, and stir in the peas, rice, and salt. Bring to a boil again, then cover and cook for 5 minutes. Reduce the heat to low and cook for another 10–15 minutes or until the water is completely absorbed and the rice is cooked.
Remove from the heat and fluff gently with a fork to separate the grains. Cover and let stand for 5 minutes before serving.
Serve with any raita or dal of your choice, any meat dish, and a green salad.
This dish goes well with any grilled meat, meat stew, or roast.

TIP
Pulao can be prepared in advance and reheated, either in the microwave or in a preheated oven at 375°F for 15–20 minutes, before serving.

KHUMB WALA PULAO
RICE WITH MUSHROOMS
SERVES 4

4 teaspoons vegetable oil
¾-inch piece cinnamon stick
2 cardamom pods, cracked
2 bay leaves
4 whole cloves
1 medium onion, thinly sliced
1½ cups sliced mushrooms
2½ cups water
1½ cups basmati rice, rinsed and drained
1½ teaspoons salt, or to taste

Heat the oil in a pan over medium heat. Stir in the cinnamon, cardamom, bay leaves, and cloves, and fry for 30 seconds. Add the onion and stir-fry until golden brown. Add the mushrooms and sauté for 5 minutes. Add the water and bring to a boil. Stir in the rice and salt. Bring to a boil again, then cover and cook for 5 minutes.
Reduce the heat to low and cook for another 7–10 minutes or until the water is absorbed completely and the rice is cooked. Remove from the heat and fluff gently with a fork to separate the grains. Cover and let stand for 5 minutes before serving. Discard whole spices.
Serve with any raita or dal, any meat dish of your choice, and a green salad.
This dish goes well with any grilled meat, meat stew, or roast.

TIP
Pulao can be prepared in advance and reheated, either in the microwave or in a preheated oven at 375°F for 15–20 minutes, before serving.

SOYA AUR SABZI PULAO
SOY AND VEGETABLE RICE
SERVES 6

¾ cup TVP granules
2 tablespoons vegetable oil
1 onion, minced
1 teaspoon ginger paste
1 teaspoon garlic paste
½ teaspoon turmeric
½ teaspoon hot chili powder or paprika
2 teaspoons salt, or to taste
1 teaspoon ground cumin
1 teaspoon garam masala (page 122)
2 medium tomatoes, chopped
3½ cups water
1 cup small cauliflower florets
1 cup sliced carrots
1½ cups basmati rice, rinsed and drained
2 tablespoons lemon juice

Prepare the TVP (see page 120). Set aside. Heat the oil in a pan over medium heat. Add the onion and sauté until golden brown. Stir in the ginger and garlic pastes, all the dry spices, and tomatoes. Stir-fry for a minute. Add the prepared TVP and stir-fry for 2–3 minutes longer. Add the water and bring to a boil. Cover and cook for 5 minutes.

Stir in the vegetables, rice, and lemon juice. Bring to a boil again, then cover, reduce the heat to low, and continue cooking for 15–20 minutes or until the rice is cooked and the water is absorbed. Remove from the heat, fluff with a fork, and let stand for 5 minutes before serving.

This dish makes a healthy and nutritious meal by itself, especially for vegetarians, but to enhance the nutritive value further, serve it with a small bowl of plain yogurt and a green salad.

TIP

Pulao can be prepared in advance and reheated, in a microwave or in a preheated oven at 375°F for 15–20 minutes, just before serving.

YAKHNI PULAO
RICE COOKED IN RICH STOCK AND MILK
SERVES 6

1 cup (or more) low-fat milk
2 tablespoons vegetable oil
1 medium onion, minced
1 teaspoon minced garlic
1 teaspoon minced fresh ginger
2 cups basmati rice, rinsed and drained
yakhni (stock)
1¾ pounds small lamb chops
4 cups water
1-inch piece cinnamon stick
3 cardamom pods, cracked
4 whole cloves
6 whole peppercorns
3 bay leaves
2 medium onions, coarsely chopped
1 teaspoon coarsely chopped garlic
2 teaspoons salt, or to taste

First make the stock: Place all the ingredients in a heavy pan and bring to a boil over medium heat. Reduce the heat and cook for about 45 minutes or until the meat is cooked. Strain and discard all the whole spices. Remove the chops from the stock, discard the bones, and set aside. Add enough milk to the stock to make 4 cups of liquid. Set aside.

Heat the oil in a pan over medium heat. Add the onion, garlic, and ginger, and sauté until golden. Add the lamb and stir-fry for 5–7 minutes. Add the milk and stock mixture and the rice, and bring to a boil. Cover and cook for 5–7 minutes.

Reduce the heat to low and cook, covered, for another 15 minutes or until the liquid is fully absorbed and the rice is cooked. Remove from the heat and let the pulao stand for 10 minutes. Fluff with a fork.

Serve with plain yogurt and pudina chutney (page 123).

TIP

Yakhni pulao can be prepared in advance and reheated, in a microwave or in a preheated oven at 375°F for 15–20 minutes, before serving.

YAKHNI PULAO

HARA PULAO

HARA PULAO

RICE WITH GREEN HERBS

SERVES 4

2 tablespoons vegetable oil
1 medium onion, minced
½ teaspoon ginger paste
½ teaspoon garlic paste
salt, to taste
2 tablespoons minced cilantro
1 tablespoon minced fresh mint leaves
2½ cups water
2 tablespoons plain, low-fat yogurt, well whisked
1½ cups basmati rice, rinsed and drained

Heat the oil in a pan over medium heat. Add the onion and stir-fry until golden brown. Add the ginger and garlic pastes, salt, cilantro, and mint, and sauté for 30 seconds. Add the water and yogurt, and bring to a boil. Stir in the rice. Bring to a boil again, then cover and cook for 5 minutes.

Reduce the heat to low and cook for another 7–10 minutes or until the water is absorbed completely and the rice is cooked. Remove from the heat and fluff gently with a fork to separate the grains. Cover and let stand for 5 minutes before serving.

Serve with any lamb or vegetarian main dish, accompanied by a vegetable or yogurt side dish.

This dish goes well with a lamb or beef roast, grilled lamb chops, or fish.

TIP

Hara pulao can be prepared in advance and reheated, in a microwave or in a preheated oven at 375°F for 15–20 minutes, before serving.

SABZI KI BIRYANI

VEGETABLE BIRYANI

SERVES 6

2 cups basmati rice
a few saffron strands, crushed (or 3–4 drops yellow
food coloring if saffron is not available)
2 tablespoons hot milk
¾ cup plain, low-fat yogurt
2 teaspoons garlic paste
1 teaspoon ginger paste
1 teaspoon ground cumin
½ teaspoon hot chili powder, or to taste
1 teaspoon garam masala (page 122)
2 tablespoons ground almonds
1 tablespoon cooking oil
2 tablespoons unsalted butter
2 medium onions, thinly sliced
4 whole cloves

2 bay leaves
¾-inch piece cinnamon stick
3 cardamom pods, cracked
4 whole peppercorns
1 small green chili pepper, chopped (optional)
1 cup cauliflower florets
1 cup sliced carrots
¾ cup frozen green peas, thawed
1 cup green beans, cut into ¾-inch pieces
1 tablespoon cashew nuts
2 tablespoons raisins
salt, to taste
2 tablespoons chopped cilantro
melted butter, for greasing the pan

Cook the rice in sufficient boiling water with a little salt until half-cooked (see page 81). Drain thoroughly. Transfer to a mixing bowl and let cool.
Soak the crushed saffron in the hot milk and set aside. Place the yogurt, garlic and ginger pastes, ground cumin, chili powder, garam masala, and ground almonds in a mixing bowl and beat thoroughly. Set aside.
Heat the oil and butter in a pan over medium heat. Add the onions and fry until golden brown. Lower the heat. Remove half the browned onion with a slotted spoon and place it in a small bowl.
Add all the whole spices to the remaining fried onions in the pan and stir-fry for 30 seconds. Stir in the chili pepper (if using), all the vegetables, cashew nuts, raisins, and salt. Increase the heat to medium and stir-fry for about 5 minutes. Stir in the yogurt mixture and bring to a boil. Reduce the heat and continue to stir-fry for 8–10 minutes. Remove from the heat and set aside.
Mix together the reserved fried onion and the cilantro, and set aside. Grease a pan with melted butter and evenly spread half the cooked rice in it. Pour the vegetable mixture over the rice, then spread the onion and cilantro mixture on top. Cover with the remaining rice and sprinkle with the milk and saffron mixture. Cover first with foil and then with a tight lid. Cook over medium-low heat for about 10–15 minutes. Remove from the heat and let stand for 20 minutes. Before serving, mix gently with a fork, then transfer to a serving dish.

When served with kachoomber raita (page 79), this is a perfect meal.

Another attractive way to serve it is to unmold the biryani onto the serving dish.

FOR BAKING
Preheat the oven to 400°F.
Grease the bottom of a suitable baking dish with melted butter and layer the rice and vegetables as above. Cover first with foil and then with a tight-fitting lid. Bake for about 15–20 minutes and serve garnished with the onion and cilantro mixture.

GOSHT BIRYANI
MEAT BIRYANI
SERVES 6

1½ pounds boneless lamb, cut into small cubes
enough vegetable oil to fry onions
2 medium onions, finely sliced
2 tablespoons raisins
2 tablespoons blanched, slivered almonds
1 teaspoon saffron strands, crushed
2 tablespoons hot milk
2½ cups basmati rice, rinsed and drained
1 teaspoon salt, or to taste
1 large onion, coarsely chopped
3–4 garlic cloves, chopped
1 teaspoon chopped fresh ginger
3 tablespoons water
2 tablespoons butter

¾-inch piece cinnamon stick
½ teaspoon cardamom seeds
½ teaspoon whole peppercorns
2 teaspoons cumin seeds
2 teaspoons coriander seeds
pinch of grated nutmeg
1 hard-boiled egg, shelled and sliced
marinade
1 cup plain, low-fat yogurt, well whisked
2 teaspoons garlic paste
1 teaspoon ginger paste
meat tenderizer, quantity as per label instructions
1½ teaspoons salt, or to taste
1 teaspoon hot chili powder or paprika

Place the lamb with all the marinade ingredients in a mixing bowl and combine thoroughly. Cover and let marinate for at least an hour.

Heat the oil in a wok or pan over medium heat and fry the sliced onions until golden brown and crisp. Remove with a slotted spoon and spread on paper towels. To the same oil, add the raisins. Remove them as soon as they swell (almost immediately) and place on paper towels. Fry half the slivered almonds for a few seconds until golden and place on paper towels. Remove the pan from the heat. Soak the saffron in the hot milk and set aside. Cook the rice in sufficient water until half-cooked. Drain, then spread it on a large platter and sprinkle with a little salt.

Blend the chopped onion, garlic, ginger, remaining slivered almonds, and 3 tablespoons of water until smooth. Heat 1 tablespoon of the oil from the onion pan with the butter in a heavy-bottomed pan over medium heat. Add the whole spices and seeds, and sauté for 10 seconds. Add the onion and almond mixture, and stir-fry until golden brown. If the onion sticks, sprinkle with a little water and continue stir-frying. Stir in the marinated lamb and nutmeg, and cook, stirring, until it starts to bubble.

Reduce the heat to low, cover the pan tightly, and cook for 45–60 minutes or until the lamb is tender and about a cup of sauce remains. Remove from the heat. Preheat the oven to 300°F.

To layer the biryani, use an ovenproof dish with a tight-fitting lid. Spoon some sauce from the cooked lamb into the bottom of the dish. Next spread half the cooked rice over and top it with the lamb and sauce. Sprinkle with the fried onions (saving a little for garnish) and top with the remaining rice. Spoon the saffron mixture over the rice. Cover the dish first with foil and then with the lid. Bake in the middle of the oven for an hour. Remove from the oven and let stand for a few minutes. Before serving, gently stir the biryani. Serve on a platter, garnished with the sliced egg, fried raisins, almonds, and onions.

Serve with tarka dal (page 59) and kachoomber raita (page 79).

TIP
This dish can be prepared a day or two in advance, up to the layering stage, and refrigerated. Bake when needed. Chicken (without tenderizer), beef, or veal can be used instead of lamb.

BREADS

Bread is an essential part of an Indian meal, particularly in the north. There are several different types of bread, mostly unleavened (without yeast).

Most Indian breads are made with very finely ground whole-wheat flour, known as *atta*, and are cooked on a *tawa* (a concave, heavy iron plate) or griddle, deep-fried, or baked in a tandoor (clay oven).

Unfortunately I have not been able to find a really good substitute for Indian atta. I have tried using whole-wheat flour, but the bread does not come out as soft as bread made with atta. By experimenting with a combination of finely sifted whole-wheat flour and all-purpose flour, I have had better results, with the bread being much softer and better-looking. Naturally, some of the vital nutrients are lost without the proper flour, and if you do have access to an Indian market, it is advisable to buy roti atta or roti flour.

BREADS

POORI

The dough for pooris is harder in consistency than that for chapatis and parathas, and a little oil or ghee is added to the flour. Poori is also generally smaller in size and rolled slightly thicker. It is deep-fried in hot oil and should puff up into small, crisp balls, although they are quite soft when eaten and taste best when hot. We fry pooris in a *karahi*—an Indian version of a wok—but any suitable deep saucepan can be used. The rolled pooris are covered with a damp cloth, waxed paper, or plastic wrap to keep them from drying out before cooking. Once the oil is hot, they can be fried very quickly.

CHAPATI (Also known as roti or phulka)

This everyday bread, eaten by most Indians, is the thinnest of the breads. It takes a little practice to make reasonably decent chapatis! The dough is made simply with flour and water, sometimes with a little salt added to the flour. The dough should be soft but not sticky, which makes rolling much easier (use extra flour while rolling to avoid sticking).

A tawa is traditionally used for making chapatis, but you can use a griddle or heavy frying pan instead. The chapati is first toasted on both sides on the preheated tawa and then "inflated" directly over burning charcoal or a gas burner. Chapatis taste best straight off the fire, although this is, of course, not always possible. At my home in Johannesburg, I stack chapatis one on top of the other, then wrap six to ten of them in plastic wrap and freeze them for later use. Microwaved or heated in the oven, they taste as good as if they were fresh. Some people like to spread them with a little butter or ghee as soon as they are made.

PARATHA

Like chapati, this is an unleavened bread, but it is shallow-fried and has rich, flaky layers. Traditionally a little oil, butter, or ghee is added to the flour before making the dough, although I omit this to cut down on fat and unnecessary calories.

Parathas are surprisingly easy to make at home. The dough is made in the same way as for chapatis, although unlike a chapati, a paratha can be rolled into different shapes, such as triangles, squares, or circles, and is slightly thicker than a chapati. It is cooked in the same way as a chapati, but a little oil or ghee is applied to both sides while cooking.

Parathas can be frozen and reheated. They are occasionally served in place of chapatis, or at breakfast with fried eggs and raita or plain yogurt.

NAAN

Naan is a leavened flatbread from northern India, made with white flour. Traditionally, it is baked in a very hot tandoor (clay oven), but these are restricted to restaurants now. I cook naan in a conventional oven and under the broiler, and the result is fairly acceptable. There are different recipes and methods for making naan. The method that I use (page 105) is easy to follow and the result is quite authentic.

Naan can be served with any vegetarian or meat dish, especially tandoori specialties.

TIPS FOR MAKING INDIAN BREAD

1. Sift the flour before measuring it.
2. Do not add all the water at once. The amount of water may have to be adjusted a little depending on the type of flour you are using.
3. We generally knead bread dough by hand, but a food processor can be used instead.
4. Always make sure that the tawa or griddle is not so hot that it burns the bread. It is advisable to keep the heat on the low side. Chapatis and parathas cook very fast and need to be turned about three times.
5. Always rest the dough for about half an hour before rolling.
6. Roll chapatis, parathas, or pooris first, spread them over the counter without overlapping, and cover them with a damp dishcloth to keep them from drying out before cooking.
7. Stack cooked chapatis or parathas as they are made and wrap them in a napkin if they will be eaten the same day, or in foil or plastic wrap for later. They freeze well and stay fresh for months.

POORI

DEEP-FRIED BREAD

MAKES 16

1⅓ cups roti flour (whole-wheat flour)
1⅓ cups all-purpose flour
½ teaspoon salt
1 tablespoon vegetable oil

¾ cup cold water
¼ cup flour, for dusting
vegetable oil, for deep-frying

Combine the flours, salt, and oil in a mixing bowl and rub together well. Gradually add the cold water and knead the dough to a hard consistency. Knead for 5 minutes more, then cover with a damp dishcloth or plastic wrap and let the dough rest for at least 30–40 minutes.

Divide the dough into sixteen equal portions and shape each into a small ball. Work with one portion at a time, keeping the rest covered with a damp cloth or plastic wrap. Take one ball, flatten it slightly with your fingertips, and roll it out on a floured pastry board with a rolling pin. Dust as needed with flour to prevent sticking. Each rolled poori should be about 2½ inches in diameter. Roll all the pooris, then spread them over the counter and cover with a damp dishcloth to keep them from drying out.

Heat sufficient oil in a deep-frying pan or wok over medium-high heat. It is important that the oil is really hot before you start frying the pooris. Drop one poori at a time into the hot oil. As it comes up, turn it over immediately and keep pressing it down to puff it up. (The whole process of frying only takes a few seconds.) The fried poori should be a nice golden color. Lift the poori out with a slotted spoon and allow the oil to drain off.

Place on a platter lined with paper towels to absorb any excess oil. Fry all the pooris in the same way and place on the platter without stacking.

Pooris taste best when served hot and are often served with vegetarian dishes.

CHAPATI
PLAIN FLATBREAD
MAKES 15

2 cups roti flour (whole-wheat flour)
½ cup all-purpose flour
a pinch of salt

1 cup warm water
¼ cup flour, for dusting

In a mixing bowl, place the roti flour, all-purpose flour, and salt in a heap. Make a well in the center and gradually add the warm water, 1–2 tablespoons at a time, while stirring from the center, kneading well to make a soft and pliable dough that leaves the bowl clean. Cover the dough with a damp dishcloth or plastic wrap and let it rest for 30–40 minutes.

Knead again with moist hands for a couple of minutes. The dough should now spring back when pressed with a finger. Divide the dough into fifteen equal portions and shape each one into a round ball. Work with one at a time, while keeping the rest covered with a damp cloth or plastic wrap. Take one ball, flatten it slightly with your fingertips, and roll it out on a floured pastry board with a rolling pin. Dust frequently with flour to avoid sticking.

Each rolled chapati should be about 5 inches in diameter. Spread the rolled chapatis on the counter as you go along, covering them with a damp dishcloth to keep them from drying out.

Heat a griddle or frying pan over medium-low heat for 5–7 minutes, and then turn the heat to low. Pick up a rolled chapati, shake off any excess flour, and place it on the preheated griddle or frying pan. Cook until the underside is dry and develops small, white spots, and small blisters start appearing on the top. Turn the chapati over and cook on the other side until golden-brown spots appear. Turn again, pressing the outer edge with a folded cloth, and it should start to inflate. Very gently press the center down and the chapati should inflate into puffed bread. If this does not happen, please do not panic! It will come with a little practice. A cooked chapati that has not inflated tastes just as good!

Repeat the same procedure with the remaining chapatis, wiping the griddle or frying pan in between to remove any burned flour. If you wish, you can put a little butter on top of each chapati as soon as it is made, then stack and store them (see point 7 on page 96).

TIKONA PARATHA
TRIANGULAR LAYERED FLATBREAD
MAKES 12

1½ cups roti flour (whole-wheat flour)
1 cup all-purpose flour
½ teaspoon salt
¼ cup vegetable oil or melted butter
1 cup warm water
¼ cup flour, for dusting

In a mixing bowl, place the roti flour, all-purpose flour, salt, and 1 tablespoon of oil or melted butter, and mix with your fingertips until the mixture resembles fine breadcrumbs. Make a well in the center. Gradually add 1–2 tablespoons of warm water at a time while stirring from the center, kneading well to make a soft and pliable dough that leaves the bowl clean. Let the dough rest for 30–40 minutes.

Knead again with moist hands for a couple of minutes. The dough should now spring back when pressed with a finger. Divide into twelve equal portions and shape each one into a round ball. Work with one portion at a time, keeping the rest covered with a damp cloth or plastic wrap. Take one round, flatten it slightly with your fingertips, and roll it out on a floured pastry board with a rolling pin.

Dust frequently with flour to prevent sticking. Each rolled paratha should be about 4 inches in diameter.

Using a pastry brush, sparingly apply oil or melted butter onto the surface. Sprinkle with a little flour and fold in half. Apply a little more oil or melted butter onto the surface of the folded paratha, sprinkle with a little more flour, and fold in half again to form a small triangle. Roll this triangle into a thin, larger triangle, dusting with flour as required. Make all the parathas the same way, then spread them over the counter and cover with a damp dishcloth to keep them from drying out before cooking.

Heat a griddle or frying pan over medium-low heat for 5–7 minutes, then turn the heat to low and smear the surface with a little oil or melted butter. Place a paratha on it and brush the top with oil or melted butter. When light brown spots develop on the underside, turn the paratha over and cook until more brown spots appear. The whole process takes about 2–3 minutes.

Place the cooked paratha on a plate and cover with foil. Cook all the remaining parathas in the same way and stack them under the foil. If they are not to be eaten immediately, wrap them in foil or plastic wrap. When you are ready to eat, unwrap them and warm them either in a preheated oven at 400°F for 10–15 minutes or in a microwave.

SOYA PARATHA
FLATBREAD WITH SOY PROTEIN
MAKES 8

½ cup TVP granules
2 tablespoons vegetable oil
1 medium onion, finely chopped
1 tablespoon minced fresh ginger
1 small green chili pepper, seeded and minced (optional)
1 teaspoon cumin seeds
1 teaspoon ground cumin
1 teaspoon ground coriander
1 tablespoon minced fresh dill

3 tablespoons minced cilantro
½ teaspoon garam masala (page 122)
salt, to taste
2 tablespoons lemon juice
1 cup roti flour (whole-wheat flour)
½ cup all-purpose flour
warm water for making dough
extra flour, for dusting
vegetable oil, for brushing parathas

Prepare the TVP (see page 120). Set aside. Heat the oil in a pan over medium heat. Add the onion, ginger, chili pepper (if using), and cumin seeds. Sauté for 1 minute. Stir in the prepared TVP granules, and cook, stirring, for 2–3 minutes. Add all the remaining ingredients except the flours, water, and oil, and mix well. Remove from the heat.

Put both the flours in a mixing bowl and mix thoroughly. Make a well in the center and gradually add the warm water, 1–2 tablespoons at a time, while stirring from the center, kneading well to make a soft and pliable dough that leaves the bowl clean.

Cover the dough with a damp dishcloth or plastic wrap and let it rest for 30–40 minutes. Knead again with moist hands for a couple of minutes. Divide the dough into sixteen equal portions and shape each into a round ball. Two portions will be used to make one paratha. Roll out two separate rounds at a time, like the chapati, about 2½ inches in diameter. Divide the TVP mixture into eight equal portions. Evenly spread one portion of the mixture onto one of the rolled rounds, leaving

½ inch around the edge clear. Place the other round on top of the filling. Press the edges together to seal the filling inside. Roll out to a 5-inch diameter, dusting frequently with flour to prevent sticking. Repeat with the remaining parathas.

Heat a griddle or frying pan over medium-low heat for 5–7 minutes, then turn the heat to low and smear the surface with a little oil. Place a paratha on it and brush the top with oil. When light brown spots develop on the underside, turn the paratha over and cook until brown spots appear on the other side as well. The whole process takes about 2–3 minutes.

Place the cooked paratha on a plate and cover with foil. Cook all the remaining parathas in the same way and stack them under the foil. If they are not to be eaten immediately, wrap them in foil or plastic wrap. When you are ready to eat, warm them either in a preheated oven at 400°F for 10–15 minutes or in a microwave.

VARIATION
To cut down further on fat, cook parathas like chapati, without using any oil while cooking.

SOYA PARATHA

NAAN

LEAVENED BREAD

MAKES 8 LARGE NAANS

(handwritten: 1 PKG. = 7G.)

2½ teaspoons active dry yeast
¼ cup warm water
2 teaspoons sugar
⅔ cup milk, at room temperature
⅔ cup plus 2 tablespoons plain,
low-fat yogurt, whisked
1 egg, beaten*

2 tablespoons melted, unsalted butter
4½ cups all-purpose flour
1 teaspoon baking powder
½ teaspoon salt
extra flour, for dusting
2 tablespoons vegetable oil
2 teaspoons poppy seeds

Mix the yeast, warm water, and sugar in a bowl and let stand for 3–4 minutes until it becomes frothy. Mix together the milk, yogurt, egg, and melted butter, and set aside. In a separate mixing bowl, sift together the flour, baking powder, and salt. Make a well in the center and add the yeast and the milk mixtures. Fold together all the ingredients, then knead until smooth. Cover the bowl tightly with foil or plastic wrap and leave it in a warm place for 45 minutes to 1 hour or until the dough has almost doubled its initial volume. Preheat the oven to 400°F.

Divide the dough into eight equal portions and shape each one into a round ball. Work with one portion at a time, keeping the rest covered with a damp cloth or plastic wrap. Take one round, flatten it slightly with your fingertips, and roll it out on a floured pastry board with a rolling pin. Pull one edge to give the naan a tear shape, which should be about 10 inches long and about 6 inches wide at the widest point. Brush the top surface with a little oil or melted butter, sprinkle with a few poppy seeds, and place on a greased baking sheet. Roll all the naans, then bake in the preheated oven for 10–12 minutes. Wrap in napkins to keep warm, and serve hot.

To store them longer, see point 7 on page 96.

* An extra ¼ cup of yogurt can be substituted for the egg.

FOR THE SWEET TOOTH

I find Indian sweets and desserts too rich and time-consuming to prepare and tend not to serve them with daily meals. Instead, meals can be rounded off with seasonal fresh fruits, of which there is an unlimited variety in India. For the calorie-conscious, it is also best to serve fresh fruit and save sweet indulgences for special occasions only.

Desserts are served at religious functions, weddings, and other festive events. Fortunately, there is a huge variety of sweets readily available at *halvai* (candy) stores in India, and it is not necessary to spend hours making them.

Most desserts are milk-based, with generous amounts of nuts and dried fruits, particularly raisins. I have also provided recipes for a few sweet drinks, which go very well with any spicy meal and which can be served in place of dessert.

Desserts in this chapter are not difficult to make and were chosen because the ingredients are readily available. They can be prepared beforehand, then refrigerated or frozen.

SOOJI KA HALVA
SEMOLINA DESSERT
MAKES 8

Indian children love this halva.

2¼ cups water
½ cup plus 2 tablespoons sugar
¼ teaspoon cardamom seeds, pounded
3 tablespoons vegetable oil
3 tablespoons unsalted butter
¾ cup coarse semolina
¼ cup raisins
¼ cup slivered almonds
1 tablespoon finely slivered pistachio nuts

Place the water, sugar, and cardamom in a saucepan and bring to a boil over medium heat. Turn the heat to low and simmer for 2 minutes. Remove from the heat and set aside. Heat the oil and butter in a large, nonstick frying pan or wok over medium heat. Add the semolina, stir, and sauté until the semolina turns a light golden color (not brown). Add the raisins and almonds, and stir for 30 seconds longer. While stirring continuously, gradually pour in the sugar mixture. Reduce the heat, continuing to stir, and cook the halva for 6–8 minutes or until it is thick and pulls away from the sides of the pan. Remove from the heat. Spread evenly in a shallow dish (such as a tart pan), sprinkle with the pistachio nuts, and let cool for 10–15 minutes. Cut into squares or diamond shapes and serve hot, warm, or at room temperature, but not chilled.

TIP
The halva can be refrigerated for 3–4 days. Warm it up in the microwave before serving.

GAJJAR KA HALVA
CARROT PUDDING
SERVES 8

This halva is a great favorite during the winter months and is often served at functions such as weddings.

5 cups milk
2¼ pounds (about 9 cups) carrots, grated
1 teaspoon cardamom seeds, pounded
½ cup ricotta cheese, crumbled
3 tablespoons vegetable oil
4 tablespoons unsalted butter
3 tablespoons raisins
3 tablespoons slivered almonds
¾ cup sugar
a generous pinch of grated nutmeg
1 tablespoon chopped almonds

Bring the milk to a boil in a suitable heavy-based pan over medium heat. Add the carrots and cardamom, and bring to a boil again. Reduce the heat and cook, stirring frequently, until no liquid remains. Stir in the ricotta cheese, oil, and butter. Stir and cook for 5 minutes.

Add all the remaining ingredients, except the chopped almonds, and continue to stir and cook for another 10 minutes or until the halva starts to draw away from the sides of the pan. Remove from the heat.

Arrange in a serving dish and garnish with the chopped almonds.

Hot halva served with a scoop of vanilla ice cream is absolutely delicious.

TIP
Gajjar ka halva stays fresh for weeks if refrigerated.

GAJJAR KA HALVA

KHEER

INDIAN FLAVOR

KHEER
RICE PUDDING
SERVES 8

½ cup basmati rice*
3½ cups water
14-ounce can evaporated milk
14-ounce can sweetened condensed milk
½ teaspoon cardamom seeds, pounded
a generous pinch of grated nutmeg

½ cup seedless raisins
½ cup chopped almonds
½ cup chopped cashew nuts
1 tablespoon finely slivered pistachio nuts
1 tablespoon finely slivered almonds

Rinse and drain the rice. Bring the water to a boil in a heavy pan over medium heat. Add the rice and bring to a boil again. Lower the heat and simmer for about 25–30 minutes or until the rice is very soft. Stir in all the remaining ingredients, except for the slivered pistachio nuts and almonds, and cook, stirring, for 10–15 minutes longer or until it is thick and creamy. Remove from the heat.

Pour into a dessert bowl and sprinkle with the slivered nuts.

Serve hot in the winter and chilled in the summer. It tastes just as good either way.

* If not available, use any other good-quality long-grain rice.

NARIAL BARFI
COCONUT FUDGE
SERVES 8

½ cup water
½ cup sugar
a few strands of saffron or a little yellow food coloring

¼ teaspoon ground cardamom
3 cups dry coconut cream
2 teaspoons finely slivered pistachio nuts
2 teaspoons finely slivered almonds

Bring the water to a boil in a saucepan over medium heat. Add the sugar, saffron, and ground cardamom, and bring to a boil again, stirring continuously, until the sugar is fully dissolved. Reduce the heat to low and simmer for 2 minutes. Add the coconut and mix well.

Remove from the heat and spread evenly in a greased, flat dish. Sprinkle with the slivered nuts and press in gently. Let cool. Cut into small squares and serve.

Can also be served with morning or afternoon tea or coffee.

SWEET DRINKS

Although we have four seasons in India, our hot summer seems the longest, especially in the northern part of the country. Every household has its own favorite cold drinks, but for me there is no substitute for lassi, thandai, or nimbu pani. These drinks are nutritious, as well as tasty and easy to prepare, and served chilled, are great thirst quenchers on hot summer days. They are popular menu items in good Indian restaurants, as well. Feel free to increase or reduce the liquid ingredients to get the consistency to your liking.

MEETHI LASSI
SWEET YOGURT SHAKE
SERVES 4

4 cups plain, low-fat yogurt
¼ cup sugar, or to taste
1½ cups chilled water
1½ cups crushed ice

Place all the ingredients in a blender and blend for about a minute until frothy. Pour into chilled glasses and serve.

VARIATIONS

For mango lassi, replace the sugar with 1 cup of fresh, ripe mango pulp and follow the same method.

Savory lassi is equally popular in Indian homes. Omit the sugar and instead add salt to taste, ½ teaspoon pepper, and 1 teaspoon ground cumin or to taste, and follow the same method. Add 1 tablespoon minced fresh mint leaves, mix with a spoon, and pour into chilled glasses.

THANDAI
POPPY SEED AND ALMOND COOLER
SERVES 2

This is a very nutritious drink, full of protein, calcium, essential fatty acids, and other vitamins and minerals.

½ cup ground almonds
4 teaspoons poppy seeds
1 tablespoon melon seeds (any variety)
8 whole peppercorns
2 cups nonfat or low-fat milk
4 teaspoons sugar, or to taste
1½ cups crushed ice

Place the ground almonds, poppy seeds, melon seeds, and peppercorns in a bowl and add 1 cup of milk. Let stand for 15 minutes. Pour this mixture into a blender and add the remaining milk and sugar. Blend until smooth and creamy. Add the ice and blend for 25–30 seconds longer. Pour into chilled glasses and serve.

MANGO LASSI

MASALE WALI CHAI

NIMBU PANI

NIMBU PANI

FRESH LIME OR LEMON JUICE

SERVES 2

2 cups water
2 tablespoons sugar, or to taste
3 tablespoons fresh lime or lemon juice
2 cups crushed ice
2 lemon slices or wedges, to garnish

Mix the water and sugar, and stir until the sugar is fully dissolved. Add the remaining ingredients and mix. Serve in chilled glasses garnished with a lemon slice or wedge.

MASALE WALI CHAI

CHILLED, SPICED TEA

SERVES 4

5 cups water
4 cardamom pods, cracked
6 whole cloves
1¼-inch piece cinnamon stick
2 teaspoons tea leaves (unflavored)
¼ cup sugar, or to taste
¼ cup fresh lemon juice
2 cups crushed ice
fresh mint sprigs, to garnish

Pour the water into a saucepan and bring to a boil over medium heat. Add the whole spices and lower the heat. Cover and simmer for 5 minutes. Remove from the heat, add the tea leaves and sugar, and cover again. Let the mixture stand for another 5 minutes. Stir well until the sugar is fully dissolved. Strain into a jug, discard the spices and tea leaves, and let cool. Add the lemon juice and crushed ice, and refrigerate until required. Serve in chilled glasses garnished with sprigs of fresh mint.

Because so many Indians are vegetarians—although a small percentage may occasionally include eggs or fish in their meal plan—it is a challenging task to provide sufficient high-quality protein in a typical meal. To make food healthier and more nutritious, eat a lot of milk and milk products, such as yogurt and paneer (homemade cheese), as well as legumes and soybean products.

BASIC
RECIPES

DAHI (yogurt/curds)

Yogurt, as everybody knows, is milk fermented with a friendly bacterial culture, and it therefore has a slightly sour taste. It can be made with whole, low-fat, or nonfat milk. The nutritive value of yogurt is very similar to that of milk. It is rich in high-quality protein, calcium, phosphorus, riboflavin and other B vitamins, and fat-soluble vitamins. Those who suffer from lactose (milk sugar) intolerance are often able to tolerate yogurt better than other milk products.

Naturally fermented yogurt, or *dahi*, has been a staple food of Indians from the earliest times. No Indian meal is considered complete without a dish of yogurt. It is used in marinades for tandoori and other specialties, for thickening gravy, and to enhance flavor and texture in rice pulao.

Although commercial yogurt is readily available in Indian cities, most people prefer to make their own fresh yogurt at home. This is a daily ritual for most Indian people, and I still make my own yogurt at home every day. I used thick, plain yogurt to begin with, and it worked very well. Each batch now provides the starter culture for the next one. Once you are accustomed to the taste and texture of fresh, natural yogurt, you will not willingly compromise with commercial products. If calories are a consideration, choose low-fat or nonfat yogurt or milk.

DAHI
HOMEMADE YOGURT
MAKES 4 CUPS

4 cups low-fat milk
3 tablespoons plain yogurt

Bring the milk to a boil. Lower the heat and let simmer for 5–7 minutes. Remove from the heat and let cool until your finger can be kept immersed in it without discomfort. Place the yogurt in a suitable bowl and add 2–3 tablespoons of warm milk to it. Mix well, then add this to the rest of the warm milk. Whisk thoroughly. Pour into a suitable bowl, cover, and keep in a warm place to set for 6–8 hours or preferably overnight. After it is set, refrigerate until needed.

TIP
In winter, it is advisable to use extra yogurt, wrap it in a dishcloth, and leave it in a warm place to set.

PANEER (Homemade cheese)

Paneer is another very important ingredient in Indian cooking, and it contains all the nutrients present in milk and yogurt. It is made by coagulating or curdling milk with lemon juice, vinegar, or natural curds. Whey is then drained off and the solids are cut into cubes. These are used for making delicious and nutritionally rich dishes that are especially good for vegetarians.

Paneer is often eaten in combination with legumes and lentils to enhance the protein value of a pure vegetarian meal. I have provided many recipes using paneer in combination with bell peppers, peas, chickpeas, spinach, and so on. Paneer kabobs cooked over a charcoal grill are mouthwatering.

Though whole milk makes the best paneer, I use low-fat milk with satisfying results. I prepare a lot of paneer at one time, divide it into smaller portions, place each portion in a freezer bag, and freeze it. It stays fresh for months.

There is no substitute for fresh, homemade paneer. Glancing at the recipe, you might feel that it is too much trouble to prepare, but it really isn't. Try it once and it will soon become second nature.

PANEER
HOMEMADE CHEESE
MAKES 8 OUNCES

8 cups whole milk or 24 cups low-fat milk
(see Tip below)
¼ cup fresh lemon juice

Bring the milk to a boil over high heat. Reduce the heat to low and stir in the lemon juice. As soon as the milk is curdled and the solids separate from the liquid whey, remove from the heat. Pour the curdled mixture into a large strainer lined with cheesecloth. Let it drain without disturbing until the cheesecloth is cool enough to handle.

Tie the cheesecloth loosely and place on a chopping board. Set another board or a flat lid on top of the paneer. Place a heavy weight (such as a large cooking pot filled with water) on top. Let drain for 4–6 hours or until the paneer is firm and compact. Cut into cubes or as specified in the recipe. Frozen paneer stays fresh for months.

TIP
A quart of whole milk will yield approximately 4 ounces of paneer, whereas low-fat milk will yield less. Paneer made with whole milk is softer and creamier than that made with low-fat milk.

SOYBEAN PRODUCTS

Soybean products are the world's most efficient source of vegetable protein. Granules (TVP) and chunks (TSP) are made from high-quality, defatted soy flour.

They are easy to digest and contain almost 55% protein on a moisture-free basis, as well as all the essential amino acids required for human nutrition. They also contain significant quantities of calcium and magnesium (essential for strong bones), along with B vitamins, vitamins E and K, and iron. Being low in fat, they are especially beneficial for keeping cholesterol in check and for cardiac and diabetic patients. They are extremely beneficial for vegetarians, who should include them in their daily food plan more frequently. Growing children and pregnant and nursing women would also benefit from the inclusion of soy products in their diet.

Soy products are almost neutral in taste and as such can be added to any dish, sweet or savory. When added to meat dishes, soy increases the quantity of the dish and reduces total saturated fat. Soy is also a much more economical option than other proteins such as meat, milk, and eggs.

PREPARING DRY SOY PROTEIN

Follow the instructions on the label, if there are any, or soak the granules or chunks for 10–15 minutes in enough hot water to swell the granules to almost three times their dry volume and the chunks to about double their dry volume. Squeeze and rinse them with fresh water 2–3 times, then squeeze out the water and discard it. The granules or chunks are now ready for use.

TOFU (Soybean curd)

We associate tofu with paneer because of its texture and appearance. It is high in protein, and a rich source of calcium and other minerals and vitamins.

Tofu is low in saturated fats and has no cholesterol at all. It is also low in calories compared to eggs and meat, and is an ideal food for the weight-conscious. As more and more people are becoming vegetarians, tofu and other soy products are being used more often in everyday foods.

Tofu is readily available at supermarkets. It is a very versatile product and can be used for making various delicious Indian dishes. Tofu can also be easily frozen for a long time, although its texture becomes a little chewy.

TSP CHUNKS

TVP GRANULES

TOFU

TANDOORI MASALA
MAKES ABOUT 1½ CUPS

**This is used in all tandoori preparations and
a few other dishes.**

1 cup cumin seeds
½ cup coriander seeds
2 teaspoons fenugreek seeds*
½ teaspoon carum seeds*
8 green cardamom seeds, removed from pods
10 whole cloves
2 teaspoons whole black peppercorns
1 teaspoon ground mace
1 teaspoon fennel seeds
4 bay leaves
¾-inch piece cinnamon stick

Grind all the spices to a fine powder. Store in an
airtight jar and refrigerate. It will stay fresh
for months.

*Though they impart a very distinctive aroma to
tandoori preparations and can be found at Indian
markets, you can omit them if they are unavailable.

TIP
Typically, most tandoori dishes are a deep orange or
reddish in appearance. This is achieved by adding
food coloring at the time of marinating. Personally,
I prefer not to use artificial coloring, but you may
wish to. If so, combine a few drops each of
red and yellow food coloring for a bright
orange color.

GARAM MASALA
MAKES ABOUT 2 CUPS

1¼ cups cumin seeds
¾ cup coriander seeds
2 teaspoons green cardamom seeds
2 teaspoons black cardamom seeds*
1 tablespoon whole cloves
two 1¼-inch pieces cinnamon stick
2 tablespoons whole black peppercorns, or to taste
4–5 bay leaves
⅛ nutmeg kernel

Grind all the spices to a fine powder. Store in an
airtight jar and refrigerate. It stays fresh for months.

* If not available, use green cardamom seeds instead
  (i.e. 4 teaspoons green cardamom seeds).

TIP
You can add this to almost any dish, especially meat
dishes with gravy. It has a very strong flavor,
however, and should be used sparingly.

TOASTED GROUND CUMIN

I use this in many dishes because of its wonderful
aroma. It is especially good in yogurt side dishes
and is very easy to prepare.

2–3 tablespoons cumin seeds

Dry-fry the cumin seeds in a small frying pan until
they turn dark brown. Let them cool, then grind them
into a fine powder in a coffee grinder. Store in an
airtight container.

ALMOND AND CASHEW NUT PASTE

Although nuts such as almonds, pistachios, and cashews are mostly used in Indian desserts and candies, they are sometimes used in savory preparations to enhance the taste and texture. Keep a small stock of nuts handy or just buy them as needed. I have used almond and cashew paste in many recipes in this book. The paste is not usually available at any supermarket or Indian market, so I grind the paste myself. Just soak the nuts in water for a while, then process in a food processor. Use fresh or prepare extra and freeze in small plastic bags for convenience.

PUDINA CHUTNEY

MINT CHUTNEY
MAKES ABOUT ¾ CUP

2 cups packed fresh mint leaves, washed
¼ cup cilantro leaves, washed
1 small onion, coarsely chopped
2 teaspoons chopped fresh ginger
1 teaspoon chopped garlic
1 tablespoon lemon or lime juice, or to taste
2 small green chili peppers (optional)
1½ teaspoons ground cumin
2 teaspoons sugar (optional)
salt, to taste

Place all the ingredients in a blender and blend until smooth. Remove to a bowl and adjust the seasoning according to taste. Tastes best when fresh. Store in a jar and refrigerate. It stays fresh for up to a week.

VARIATION
1 small, raw mango (if in season) can be substituted for the lemon or lime juice. Peel the mango, discard the pit, and blend it with the other ingredients.

DAHI PUDINA CHUTNEY

YOGURT MINT CHUTNEY
MAKES ABOUT 1¾ CUPS

1 quantity pudina chutney (see recipe below)
1 cup plain, low-fat yogurt, whisked
1 tablespoon lime juice
½ teaspoon pepper
½ teaspoon hot chili powder
2 teaspoons sugar
salt, to taste

Place all the ingredients in a bowl and mix well. Adjust seasoning. Chill and use fresh.

SERVING SUGGESTIONS
Serve with all tandoori dishes, such as murgi ka tikka and boti kabob, and some appetizers, such as chana bhajia or sabzi pakora.
    Serve as a dip with potato or tortilla chips.

GLOSSARY
OF HERBS AND SPICES

The following herbs and spices are referred to in many of the recipes in this book. The majority of them are readily available at large supermarkets, while some of them (marked with an *) may have to be purchased from an Indian or Asian market.

It is preferable to buy small quantities of spices at a time and store them in airtight containers in a cool place or in the refrigerator, where they will stay fresh for months.

Bay leaf
Tej patta
Bay leaf is an aromatic herb used in many Indian meat dishes, rice pulao, and biryani. It can be purchased in dried leaf or powder form.

Black peppercorn
Kali mirch
Black peppercorns have a pleasant, distinctive flavor and are mildly pungent in taste. They are used whole in some preparations or in powder form, freshly ground if possible.

Black salt*
Kala namak
This is not really black in color as the name suggests, but closer to deep purple. It has a strong, unusual flavor and is excellent in yogurt dishes, raita, and savory snacks. It can be found at most Indian markets, and is preferably bought in powder form.

Cardamom—green and brown*
Choti elichi and kali elichi
Cardamom has dried, small green pods or large, dark brown pods, with aromatic seeds inside. The seeds are used in meat and poultry dishes, rice pulao, or biryani, and for flavoring desserts. Cardamom is also used for making masala chai tea with aromatic spices and garam masala. It is available as whole pods, seeds, or as a powder.

Carum seeds*
Ajwain
These very tiny, light brown seeds have a flavor similar to that of thyme, but are very bitter. Carum is an important ingredient in tandoori cooking, masala, and some Indian breads. It is available at Indian markets.

Chili powder
Lal mirchi powder
Often extremely pungent and fiery, chili powder's heat varies according to the variety. It should be used with caution and the quantity adjusted to taste. Cayenne pepper or paprika can be used as an alternative.

Cilantro
Hara dhania
This herb has a lovely fragrance. It is used extensively for making delicious chutneys and dips, and for garnishing.

Cinnamon
Dalchini
Available in powder form or as bark, cinnamon is sweet and aromatic. It is used in rice preparations, some meat dishes, and for making garam masala.

Cloves, whole
Long
Like cinnamon, cloves have a sweet aroma but are bitter to the taste. They are used in many savory dishes and for making garam masala.

Coriander seeds
Sabat dhania
These aromatic seeds are used either coarsely ground or in powder form. They are an important ingredient in masalas and vegetable dishes.

Cumin
Zeera
These small, oval-shaped, light brown seeds have small ridges and resemble caraway seeds. They are strongly aromatic and are readily available whole or in powder form.

Fennel seeds
Saunf
Fennel seeds are long, small, shaped like rice, and green in color, with a pleasant, sweetish fragrance. They're used as flavor-enhancers and also as a mouth-freshener after meals.

Fenugreek*
Methi seeds
An important and commonly used spice in India, Greece, and Egypt, fenugreek has small, hard seeds, brownish yellow in color. They have a strong aroma, are slightly bitter in taste, and are excellent in tandoori masala and other dishes.

Garlic
Lahsun
Raw garlic has a strong flavor, but cooking enhances and softens it. It is indispensable in most north Indian dishes, especially meat.

Ginger, fresh
Adrak
Essential for various Indian recipes, it provides a distinctive flavor to meat and some vegetable dishes. Choose golden-brown, fresh-looking ginger.

If stored in an airtight container and refrigerated, it will stay fresh for several days. It can also be frozen.

Mace
Javitri
Used for many Indian meat dishes, mace is a web-like, brownish-red aril that surrounds the kernel of nutmeg. It has a distinctive flavor and is not as strong as nutmeg.

Nutmeg
Jaifal
Nutmeg has a subtle, sweet flavor, used in savory and sweet dishes.

Saffron
Kesar
Probably the most expensive spice, it is available in dried strands. It has a slightly bitter, distinctive flavor and gives a pleasing yellow color to food. Saffron is much used in northern India for savory and sweet dishes.

Turmeric
Haldi
Available as a powder, it is aromatic and slightly bitter in taste. Used in most Indian dishes for color and flavor.

INDEX